Praise for 4 Minut

The most impactful spiritual practice I've implemented in the last decade is 4 Minutes. This book influenced our family so much…we actually have "Got 4 Minutes?" on a whiteboard in our kitchen. Four hours in prayer used to feel like the gold standard, but knowing God can speak to us in four minutes is a game changer the world needs to know about.

—Ryan Leak, Executive Coach, Speaker & Author

Me Ra's story is one of diving listening. As someone who doesn't practice a religion, but who believes deeply that religion and spiritual practices are inherently beautiful, I found these pages insightful, glorious, and beautiful. I love that she not only brings light to her faith but also a willingness to find meaning in it. That is the most inspiring thing of all. This book teaches us that if we are open to others, to ourselves, and to our impact in the world, we can and will create a life of meaning and purpose.

—Brooke Shaden, Artist, Fine Art Photographer, Speaker & Philanthropist, @brookeshaden

Everyone needs to hear the voice of their Father in heaven, especially the brokenhearted. This book is a nonreligious practical approach to trusting your reliance on knowing that this amazing God will speak to you. Having a relationship with God is a two-way street. Waiting on Him to speak teaches us how God sounds. Me Ra's words instruct you in sensing God's cadence and personality.

Through the many years of our relationship with Me Ra, we've always known her to be an authentic and creative soul. It's a privilege to read and enjoy *4 Minutes to Hear God's Voice*.

We believe it will have a great impact on you.

—Mike and Kathy Hayes, Founding Pastors of Covenant Church and the Center for National Renewal

Also by Me Ra Koh

Beauty Restored

Your Baby in Pictures

Your Child in Pictures

Your Family in Pictures

Work Happily Ever-After

4
MINUTES
TO HEAR GOD'S VOICE

Me Ra Koh

Cover Design and Artwork: Jasen Roman and Brian Tausend
Interior Design: Brian Tausend
Author Photo: Me Ra Koh Portraits
Printed in the United States of America

This book is dedicated to

Pascaline and Blaze

For all our 4 Minute adventures as a family and your future ones to come. For every friend, family member, and stranger we ever met. Thank you for always doing 4 Minutes with Mom and Dad. As much as it blessed all those people, it made me and your dad prouder than words could ever express.

Anna and Shalom

For thirty years of friendship and still setting the timer for each other.

Every Reader

For all the healing, direction, and adventure that waits for you on the other side of four minutes.

Table of Contents

Part 4: Thirty Years Later

To us, waiting is wasting. To God, waiting is working.

—Louie Giglio

When Your World Is on Fire

This is my sixth book. I have never written one so fast. For the last decade, I have been writing bits and pieces of it. But on a recent family trip to Colorado, I sat down one morning to journal. Nine hours later I got up! Nine. The next day, I did another six hours. The first draft poured out of me in two days, less than fifteen hours!

My other books have taken me anywhere from one to ten years to write. This time was unlike anything I had ever experienced. I felt a burning in my fingers as I typed, and when I got up at the end of each day, my body was trembling. The way my husband and teenagers looked at me, we could feel God moving in this space. For ten years I had been asking God if I should write this book. I'd been feeling the tug of war in wanting to share but was also hesitant to share one of the most intimate parts of our family.

Why now? I'm not totally sure, but I can make some solid guesses. We're six months into COVID-19, and it has changed our world. Every time you read the headlines, the titles are things like "Record Breaking Numbers," "Coronavirus on the Rise," "Protests Turned to Looting," "Police Brutality," "West Coast Fires," "More Outbreaks, Less Room in Hospitals." The list goes on and on. Our economy has been impacted on a global level. Churches haven't been able to gather. Fear runs rampant. Second-guessing every decision has never felt more overwhelming.

My husband, Brian, and I have a family portrait studio in Frisco, Texas. It took a major hit like every other small business. We lost 90 percent of our business overnight. My mind was scrambling to come up with ways to generate revenue. Brian and I came up with a list. But which one do we focus on first? It felt like we had to hit a home run, but the game was about to get cancelled.

I wanted to relaunch some of our online photography workshops, but Brian wasn't on the same page. Whenever we can't agree, or we aren't sure about what to do, we do 4 Minutes. We set the timer for four minutes and just listen for God to give us direction. I thought, "I love the 4 Minutes! God is going to show Brian that he just needs to listen to his wife!"

At the end of our 4 Minutes, Brian sensed confirmation that we were supposed to focus on the day-to-day operations of our portrait studio, using this slow time to improve our processes. I thought, "That's not what he was supposed to hear." He said he kept telling God he was supposed to hear about whether or not to launch our online workshops, but he felt like they were in a chest that we needed to wait to open. There was something else to do first.

I felt uneasy about the picture I had, especially after hearing what Brian got. During the 4 Minutes, I had a picture of me asking our friend, a fellow speaker, how he'd feel about pitching me to speak on the 4 Minutes to churches he knew. That was not what I was expecting to hear. The idea left me feeling awkward. Brian shrugged his shoulders and said, "Why not ask him? What's it going to hurt?"

When I texted my friend (because I was too uncomfortable to even call him about this), his response was, "Where's the book?"

We had set the timer for four minutes to seek direction from God on what to do about our photography business. What I received had nothing to do with our business or how to provide for our family. It didn't feel like an answer on how to create revenue for our studio, but it was an answer on how to use my time. And under all the voices of fear and doubt, I heard God whisper a promise: "You write Me Ra, and I'll take care of your family and business." And He has.

Desperate times make me desperate to hear God's voice. I know I'm not alone in this. Many of us struggle to hear from God. When pain, fear, and doubt are rising, we sometimes feel like God is silent. If He seems silent too long, we start to question if He even cares. Does He know our names or personal situations? Can He give us direction, help us know what to do?

Introduction

These heartfelt questions are what this *4 Minutes* book is all about.

My hope is that the stories you read will bring healing, make you laugh, inspire you, challenge you, shake up your faith, give you courage to take new leaps of faith, and most of all, pull you into a place of curiosity where you find yourself setting a timer for 4 Minutes again and again.

Our world is in a season of devastation. The pain and losses we continue to experience weigh heavy on us all. For myself, I feel like there are a thousand small things to grieve. It's like everything that was familiar was taken away before we even realized it was leaving. But my spirit sees something else happening.

When the familiar is gone, there is room for something new. In nature, devastating forest fires ignite new growth. Seedlings that were once dormant are activated, as they start pushing through the charred branches to live, grow, and thrive.

Brian and I believe that God wants to move in a new way. As working artists, we are always pressing into His creativity. Artists are driven to create new things, not produce the same thing over and over again. How much more does God, the Master Creator, delight in creating new seasons and gifts for us? I hope the 4 Minutes is one of those new gifts God cultivates in your daily life.

Word of caution…when you set the timer, buckle your seat belt. Over time, this listening prayer practice will transform your spirit, marriage, family, and business. When you start taking four minutes to listen to God, you'll be blown away by what He says and where He takes you! He loves taking His people to unfamiliar places because He loves adventure.

PART 1

Shattered Hearts Made Whole

CHAPTER 1

A Different Way to Pray

My husband and I aren't pastors. We didn't go to seminary. To the outside world, we are professional photographers by trade. We've had a show on Disney and are regular guest photo experts on national morning shows. But behind the scenes, we have a passion for helping people discover that God knows their names and cares for them. We do this through a specific type of prayer that we've been practicing for thirty years. It's called 4 Minutes.

I have lost track of many of the stories we have witnessed and told that were inspired by our 4 Minutes. The story that you are about to read—this book you hold in your hands—is the greatest story Brian and I have ever written. It took thirty years to form; it crosses generations, oceans, cultures, religions, and financial barriers. It is the story that shaped our family and changed our world, and it can do the same for you.

Before Brian and I met, we both hit our greatest moments of pain. You will hear more of our personal stories in the coming pages. Even though we didn't know each other, our hearts both ached for the same thing. We were desperate to know if God was real, and if so, did He know our names? Did He see our suffering? Did He even care?

This 4 Minutes that we're going to teach you will prove again and again that God not only knows your name but He is also for you and not against you. He knows your story and where you come from and wants to help write your next chapters. This book is about how to let Him author your story with healing, adventure, dreams, and joy unfathomable. It all starts with setting the timer for four minutes.

WHAT IS 4 MINUTES?

Our family calls it 4 Minutes for short. But the long version to our practice might be something like "four minutes of listening prayer." That just sounds too spiritual for us, so we stick with "4 Minutes." You'll come to see throughout this book that we're pretty down-to-earth in all things. Simple is best.

This 4 Minutes is the simplest prayer you'll ever do. You don't have to worry about saying the right words or sounding spiritual enough. You don't even have to worry about whether or not the person you're doing 4 Minutes for shares the same theology. Why? For 4 Minutes, you're not going to say anything at all. And yet, it will change your world in endless, extraordinary ways.

Throughout this book, our family is going to share dozens of stories on how 4 Minutes took us to Egypt, and then a year later around the world. And how 4 Minutes gave us clear vision and hope for a new chapter in life and comfort and healing during seasons of pain and grief.

The 4 Minutes exercise saved our marriage and brought us closer than we could have ever imagined. The outcome has been that our kids grew up believing God not only exists, but He also loves to speak to them. And there is no greater adventure then following what you hear Him say. Imagine that being the foundation of your family culture. It would change your world. Right?

HOW DO YOU DO 4 MINUTES?

If you're like me, you want the answers right away. Most of the time, life doesn't work that way, but for this book it can! There is no magic process to 4 Minutes. The prayer is simple. It's so simple you're going to wonder if you should even keep reading.

Here it is. Ready? You set the timer for four minutes and listen. No talking, no praying in your mind, not even under your breath. Your objective is to clear your mind of all the noise and focus on listening to God's voice. You're practicing a form of active listening. What are you listening for? Pictures, words, Bible verses, quotes, and any other senses you feel like God is giving you. At the end of the 4 Minutes, you write it all down and share it with whomever you're doing it with.

That's it! Pretty straightforward, right?

If it's so easy, why don't more of us do it? If you're like me, and you aspire to do good as much as possible, this is where you might start to beat up on yourself. Let's step into grace instead. We live in a society of noise. Taking time to listen to your friend over coffee without checking your phone takes a lot of work, let alone setting the timer for four minutes to listen to God. Listening is a practice that must be practiced. It's not glamorous or super spiritual. It's downright tough when fear and doubt are swarming in your heart and head. But the reward is unending.

WHEN DO YOU DO 4 MINUTES?

We're in the Rocky Mountains of Colorado right now before our oldest goes back to college. Yesterday, our family hiked a seven-and-a-half-mile trail. The first third of the trail was tricky footing. Sharp rocks and roots protruded from the earth, and if we weren't watching our steps, we'd fall. At first, I felt frustrated because I was hiking to see the scenery. Instead, I wasn't able to see anything past the next step. Then the landscape changed. The uphill rocky, root-covered path turned into a flattened, soft dirt trail. We were surrounded by a wide-open meadow of wildflowers with mountain peaks reaching high in the background. I didn't have to look at my feet anymore. I could finally exhale and take in the view. Eventually, the trail shifted, and we were climbing again, watching every step.

Life is a lot like that trail. There are some seasons when

stress and anxiety surround you like thick, clustered trees. You can't feel the sun, and you have to measure every step you take. That's the perfect time to do 4 Minutes. In fact, whenever we feel uncertain of what to do next, that's when we set the timer for four minutes. If Brian and I are facing a tough situation in our marriage, we set the timer for four minutes. When we're not sure about how to parent the kids, we set the timer for four minutes. When our business is struggling, or we're at a major crossroads, we set the timer for four minutes. When finances are running low, and we feel like we're out of options, we set the timer for four minutes. When we don't know how to counsel or kids or friends, we set the timer for four minutes and listen for them.

Making 4 Minutes a regular practice in your daily life is one of the most freeing things you could ever do. One friend of ours told us how freed up he felt after doing 4 Minutes with us. As a pastor, he counsels married couples and families every week. A lot of the time he isn't sure what the right answer is but doing 4 Minutes set him free. He realized that he doesn't have to have all the answers. Nowadays, when people come to see him for advice, he says, "Let's listen and see what God has to say." And then he sets the timer for four minutes and together they listen.

FINDING PEACE IN LEFT FIELD

Doing 4 Minutes as a family has led us across the globe, taken us on the most unreal adventures, and through it all kept us close-knit when the world felt like it was on fire.

Throughout the process of building big dreams as a

family and with our business, we've experienced countless moments of discouragement that left us wondering if we were in left field. Feeling like you're in left field is bound to happen when you say yes to taking an adventure with God. Any time you step out in faith for your family, business, or community, you're choosing to believe in what you can't see.

When those "left field" moments get overwhelming, we know it's time to set the timer for 4 Minutes. Sometimes the four minutes goes by fast. Other times, the seconds seem to crawl by. Sometimes we all get unexpected pictures and words. Other times, one of us gets something and the rest of us get nothing. But every time, no matter what the circumstance, we always finish 4 Minutes with one guaranteed result: Peace—the kind of deep peace that passes all understanding. Not too bad for the worst-case scenario, right?

HOW OFTEN DO YOU DO 4 MINUTES?

When Brian and I got engaged, we started seeing a professional counselor right away. We both came from so much trauma that we knew we needed serious, professional help if our marriage was ever going to make it. We've had the same counselor for twenty-four years! Let me explain why.

In one of our first sessions, I asked the counselor how long he thought we needed to come. Roger smiled at me and said, "That's a great question." I thought, "Typical answer for a counselor." But Roger went on, "Me Ra, Jesus promised we'd all face storms in this life. When you are facing a storm, my door is always open to you. But when you're not in a storm, enjoy life."

His answer blew me away. I was expecting him to say,

"Let's reevaluate in six months and see how your marriage is doing." But his answer was so much wiser. That is why Roger has been in our life for twenty-four years. When storms come, his wisdom helps guide us through.

How often we do 4 Minutes is similar. There are some seasons in life when we've done 4 Minutes every morning, needing a big dose of renewed faith to endure what we were facing. Other seasons we've sat down and realized a couple months went by since we did 4 Minutes as a couple or family. It's kind of like being in that wide-open meadow enjoying the scenery and wildflowers. This listening practice isn't about frequency; it's about cultivating a lifestyle that chooses to pause when your world feels uncertain.

CROSSING CULTURAL, RELIGIOUS, SPIRITUAL, AND MARITAL BARRIERS

We've done the 4 Minutes with executives of major household brands, in bars with backpackers in Southeast Asia, with Muslims in Egypt and Jews in Israel, with friends who don't know Jesus and friends who do. We've done 4 Minutes with pastors who look like they're living their best lives but behind the scenes are burned out and on the brink of divorce. Later in the book you'll read how I did 4 Minutes when I spoke at a creative conference hosted at the largest meditation center in North America, as well as the stories of those whose pain and grief went beyond words.

I can't think of a time we've asked someone if we could do 4 Minutes for them and they said no. I think it's because the practice of being quiet with someone, listening for them, is nonthreatening. If I tell you that I'm not going to say a word while we pray, but just listen for what God wants to say to you during this 4 Minutes, what do you have to lose? This listening exercise is simple but powerful.

Within these pages, we will teach you how to do 4 Minutes, whether you are single or wanting to hear God's voice in your marriage and family. Does anyone else struggle with trying to pray with your spouse? Brian and I always did until 4 Minutes.

We'll also walk you through the steps of how to teach this listening prayer to your kids. Our kids were four and seven years old when we started 4 Minutes with them. Get ready! What kids hear God say will blow you away because they don't have years of disappointment or disillusionment to press through.

We're also going to share several examples from our own experiences of what it looks like to hear God's voice for complete strangers, your community, and your future.

Brian and I started practicing this idea of listening prayer when we were nineteen years old. Almost thirty years later, we're still learning to listen. We still experience growing pains as we stretch our faith to act on what we hear. But we are being transformed with every 4 Minutes.

As we've taught this practice to our children and friends, we've learned a handful of things along the way. If you want to learn how to hear from God in your daily life, as well as unprecedented times, buckle your seat belt! You're about to start an adventure unlike any other.

WHAT DOES IT LOOK LIKE TO HEAR FROM GOD?

This is probably one of the questions we get asked the most. Our family loves this question. All four of us are different with our own distinct personalities. It only makes sense that God would speak to each of us differently. Throughout the years, we've noticed how God gives each of us different types of pictures, words, and senses.

Brian often gets abstract pictures that are sometimes connected to things in the room around us. I've lost count of how many times his pictures didn't make any sense to me, but the moment he shares it with the person we're listening for they burst into tears. My pictures and words are often more straightforward and come in sets of two to three at a time with an exhortation of some kind. When the kids were little, they nicknamed me "Mailbox" because it's never just one letter in the mail from God but several. Pascaline often has a lot of intricate detail in her images, as well as a blend of history. Blaze is the one who takes people by surprise. As a little boy, he was the youngest and quietest in our family, but when he gets a picture for you…look out. He delivers it with such simple clarity, you can't help but wonder if he read your journal.

Hearing from God can look different for each of us. As we have made our living as professional photographers, authors, and speakers, we know firsthand how God longs to live outside of the box. We know Him as the Creator who inspires our creativity. Creativity requires a certain state of playfulness. Creativity is messy and often feels like you're groping in the dark. That's exactly what 4 Minutes feels like.

BOUNDARIES FOR 4 MINUTES

We are not prophets proclaiming, "Thus, sayeth the Lord." Our family has set boundaries to what we share and don't share:

1. We don't tell people if they should quit their jobs.
2. We never tell anyone who they should marry.
3. We're not here to tell you the sex of your baby.
4. And we don't know the winning lottery numbers. (Although, that would be nice!)

These things are not what the 4 Minutes is about. This is about learning to walk in step with the Holy Spirit, believing that God knows your name and cares. Underneath all the anxiety and pain, those big things aren't really the things people want to hear most. The brokenhearted are hungry for something much deeper.

Whatever you hear in the 4 Minutes should line up with Scripture, be test-worthy, and encourage or affirm what the person was already asking God. And it should always be delivered with a spirit of humility that starts with the words, "This is what I'm sensing, but only keep what rings true to you."

ROAD SIGNS ALONG THE WAY

As I write this, our family is taking the day off after that major hike we did in Colorado. We're staying inside, reading, and resting around the fire. During our hike, we climbed more than a thousand feet in elevation. The hardest part was that we already started at a high elevation being in the Rocky Mountains. The air is much thinner here. Within the first few days of arriving, it's not uncommon to experience altitude sickness. Yesterday, during our hike, we were all short of breath.

Our destination was a beautiful waterfall. Every time we passed a small sign that basically said, "You're going the right way," I was relieved. It's already hard enough to be in the wilderness, hiking an unknown trail at a high altitude in conditions you're not used to. No one wants to get lost on top of that. Road signs along the way mean everything.

That's what life with 4 Minutes is like. Your hopes and dreams are the destination. But you're traveling into unknown terrain. Sometimes you feel so out of sorts, it's like the air has become thinner and you can't catch your breath. Fear steps in and tells you that you've taken a wrong turn. A road sign, even a small marker, that confirms you're going the right direction means everything.

The words, pictures, senses, or Bible verses we get are like those small road signs that let us know we're headed in the right direction. Whatever our family hears during our 4 Minutes should either encourage or confirm what we're already asking or sensing. This applies to doing the 4 Minutes for other people too. If we get something that doesn't make any sense, it's okay. We're all students at trying to hear God's voice. We keep a journal to write it all down. Everything, no matter how odd, gets written down. We assume the words are for another day. Some words have taken years to make any sense. Others make sense right away.

To experience the joy and power of 4 Minutes, you have to approach it with a playful heart. Once the noise in your head quiets down, trying to hear from God will feel like you're groping in the dark. In the beginning, you will wonder if the words, pictures, and senses you're hearing are coming from your imagination or indigestion. How could it be this simple to hear from God? Setting a timer for four minutes and not saying anything? Isn't prayer supposed to be way more involved?

There are all types of prayer. This is our family's favorite way to pray. We believe God longs—downright hungers—to speak to all people. The only question is...do you have four minutes to listen? The smallest effort, even something as short as four minutes, can transform everything.

CHAPTER 2

Deep Sea Diving

The first time I went scuba diving was insane and happened in the middle of nowhere in Thailand. Brian and I had the crazy idea to bring our four- and seven-year-old to the jungle, rent an open-aired house that was only accessible by a rickety long-tail boat, and live there for six weeks with five hours of electricity a day and a cooler as our only means of refrigeration. What could go wrong?

After a few weeks, Brian and I decided we needed a break from our two kids. We decided to leave them with locals we had met. Locals who couldn't speak much English. If you've had young children, you know how desperate you can get for a break. And speaking the same language is overrated. This was our reasoning as we got on a boat and set off for our first day of scuba diving.

If I haven't lost you at this point with our early parenting skills, thank you. I recognize that as grace or just plain curiosity. Either way, you're still reading. The kids have great, entertaining stories from this. You'll have to come over for dinner, and we'll let the kids do the talking on what happened when Mom and Dad left them for the day in a jungle with local Thai people.

So, Brian and I are on this boat. I'm feeling a bit seasick and worried about not fully understanding what goes into this Discovery Dive, which is what they call your first dive when you have no idea of what you're doing.

The head diver was Australian. He informed us that Jacques was going to be our guide diver. Jacques was German and didn't speak much English. He spoke fluent German, French, and Spanish. Did we speak any of those languages? No. The Australian guy said not to worry because we weren't going to be speaking underwater anyways. I could already feel the kids getting their revenge.

Jacques used pictures and charts with hand signals to explain what we were going to do. All I could think is that I was going to die. And I barely said good-bye to my kids. He went through the regulator—how we needed to pause every two feet during our descent to equalize (or pop) our ears. And then we had to demonstrate a few skills to prove we were good to go. One of those skills was going to the bottom, filling your mask with water (Yes! Filling your mask with salty sea water while you are thirty feet under.), and then blowing the water out of your mask (while not breathing it in and dying at the bottom of the ocean).

Brian jumped in right away. He was born to scuba dive. I stood on the edge of the boat and almost peed my wet suit. I was terrified. One of the few English words Jacques knew was *jump*. He kept yelling, "Jump, Me Ra! Jump!" And I stood there and shook my head no. This was nuts! If I was honest, I didn't understand a word of what he taught us before this moment. Was I really going to end my life now?

Then Brian started yelling too. "Jump, Me Ra! Come on!" He was yelling with a big golden retriever smile on his face, as if to say, "What could possibly go wrong?" I adore that smile, but sometimes it can make me furious, especially when I can think of a million things that can go wrong.

Needless to say, I finally jumped.

Jacques swam over to me with a big smile. He grabbed the buoyancy control device to my life jacket, pushed my mask against my face to make sure it was airtight, and before I could say anything else, said, "Now we go down." Regardless of how ready or not I felt, he took all the air out of my life jacket so that I sunk into the water. We got to the bottom, and even though I was terrified to flood my mask, I did.

I'm obviously still here to tell the story. But you know what? I think God got a kick out of the whole thing.

He knows I'm not one for small talk. He knows I love to go deep sea diving with people. And that I always offer to jump first. In fact, looking back on it, that tattooed, big-bellied, chain-smoking, long-haired, greasy blonde German named Jacques was another side of God. The side of God that treads water and says, "Jump, Me Ra! Jump!"

All that to say, can we skip the shallow talk and jump right in? I'll jump first.

I believe this book is going to change your life. But for this to happen, we (meaning these pages and God) need access to your heart. I know that is a big ask on my part, especially if we've never met. That is why I'm offering to share first. I want to share one of the darkest times of my life so that you'll know you're not alone.

SHATTERED HEART

This is the kind of deep-sea diving where I tell you a part of my story that you never saw coming. The kind where my story might even take your breath away because you relate to it in some way. If you will take this risk with me, I promise we'll come up for air soon. I think it's important for you to know the state of my heart before I ever understood what it meant to hear God's voice. When you hear the humble beginnings I came from, you'll appreciate the later insane, cliff-jumping adventures that much more.

I was desperate to hear from God.

In 1991 I walked on to a Christian college campus as a freshman. After my mom and aunt finished settling me into my door room, we said our good-byes. This was my first time being on my own, and I had no idea what to expect. I was in line for the campus BBQ orientation dinner. An older student was a couple people in front of me. He was making everyone around him laugh, and I noticed that student leaders were waving to him as they passed by. It never occurred to me to wonder why he was at a freshman event since he wasn't helping. He caught my eye, introduced himself, and started talking with me while we waited in line.

I'd grown up with a Korean father and Scottish/Spanish mother: two extreme opposite cultures that don't mix well. When I turned twelve, my dad started taking out his stress on me with bursts of rage and hurtful words. Over the years, my self-esteem became nonexistent. I had zero self-worth. When this older student started paying attention to me, I was flattered. He seemed to be liked by everyone, and yet he wanted to talk to me. I felt a small hope for this new chapter in life.

I never expected to see the guy again. That is why I was thrown off when he showed up on my dorm room floor a week later. Over the next few weeks, we kept running in to each other. I learned he was studying to be a youth pastor. He was also part of the small singing group that traveled around the country to represent and promote our university. When he asked me out on an official first date, I was surprised.

At first everything was wonderful. He'd send me huge bouquets of flowers to my dorm room, and all the girls would rush in to see who it was from. Everyone thought it was amazing that I'd already met someone special. Having never dated anyone seriously, I couldn't believe it myself.

Yet, after a few months of dating, a heaviness started to settle inside me that I couldn't explain. There were moments when things were off. One night I met him in the dorm lobby before going to dinner. When he saw me, he looked me up and down and said, "Why are you wearing that? You're not going to seriously wear that to dinner?" Instead of putting my shoulders back and saying, "I like what I'm wearing." I shrunk in shame, apologized, and went back to my dorm room to change.

When we were out to dinner, he kept eyeing another woman in a business suit. He compared me to her. "Look at how she holds herself with confidence. Look at those legs." Then he'd turn and look at me, "You're nothing like that." Instead of getting up and leaving, I absorbed his painful words.

As a way of looking out for me, he told me that he heard my girlfriends talking about me behind my back. He suggested I spend less time with them since they weren't trustworthy. Without asking my girlfriends about it, I assumed he was telling the truth and started to pull out of all my friendships.

Within a short time, I found myself completely isolated with him as my only friend. Whatever he suggested, I did. It wasn't that I lost my voice; I had never known I had a voice before him. And the bullying, hurtful dynamic of our dating relationship felt all too familiar with how I grew up.

Yet, I somehow managed to stop dating him. After several months I broke it off and hoped that sinking feeling inside me would go away. He was confident that God told him we were supposed to be married. That statement was intimidating since he was the one studying to be a youth pastor. Was I disappointing God too? Even though we weren't dating, he was persistent about us remaining friends and spending some time together. After weeks of him asking to have dinner, I finally said yes. It was Valentine's day.

Dinner was horrible. He was rude to the waitress and critical of me. When we left, he asked if he could drive my car and take me back to the college. Except he didn't take me back. He took me to an abandoned parking lot where he raped me.

I remember the struggle, the moment I gave up, and the tears. So many tears.

He dropped me off at my dorm and said, "Hey, I'll see you later this week!" as if nothing had happened. I stepped into the shower with all my clothes on and cried. I felt so dirty but kept thinking about how he'd left me—as if nothing had happened. Had anything happened? Maybe I was going crazy.

Over the next few months, he kept his distance. And I started to change. I wore dark-colored, baggy clothes to hide my figure. My grades started falling, but I didn't seem to notice. Life felt like a thick fog until someone woke me up.

A resident assistant approached me. The sun was out and warm against my shoulders as I listened to her. She explained that her dorm had hosted a representative from the Seattle Sexual Assault Center. The speaker shared the different characteristics of someone who has been date raped. "And you seem to exhibit them all. Me Ra, has something happened?"

I felt like someone threw icy water on my face, and I woke up to the nightmare I'd been avoiding. When I told her what happened, she confirmed that it was date rape. But I was a virgin. I had been saving myself for my husband. This kind of thing wasn't supposed to happen to me. And yet, it had.

We called the police, and I reported the incident, feeling like the rape was happening all over again with each question I answered. The police officer suggested I obtain a restraining order. If that went well, I should keep pursuing my case. I nodded, feeling like I was watching someone else's life.

The next year was one of the darkest times of my life. I wasn't in the dorm and lived out of my car, couch surfing from one friend's apartment to the next. And since rape is less about sex and more about power and control, my ex-boyfriend stalked me in every way possible.

My phone rang randomly through all hours of the night. He asked casual friends if they knew what I was doing over the weekend. When I'd walk into a restaurant for lunch, he'd already be sitting at his own table. He was trying to send me a constant message that I would never be rid of his control. And it was working.

In court, I was denied a restraining order. I didn't know that I needed a lawyer, but he knew and brought the best in Seattle with twenty people from his church to support him in the audience. Shame strangled me as I recounted every detail of that night in front of a courtroom of people who didn't believe me. I insisted that my mom stand outside of the courtroom because I didn't want her to hear the details of what had happened, but I could see her face through the glass window.

The woman judge looked at me and asked, "If it was so bad, why didn't you just get out of the car?" I didn't know what to say. Restraining order denied. Case closed. He would be allowed to stay enrolled as a student at our university. Innocent until proven guilty. I will never forget looking at my mom through the glass window and seeing the tears roll down her face. She could tell I had lost before I even finished responding to the judge, and we both felt helplessness swallow us whole.

WHAT I NEEDED MOST

During this season I found Seattle Vineyard Christian Fellowship. This church was like an emergency room for the brokenhearted. The pastor was a recovering alcoholic and went around Seattle putting up signs that read, "Alcoholics, Drug Users, Abused, AIDS victims, come as you are to Seattle

Vineyard on 42nd and Brooklyn." The church building was a converted bar, and between those signs and return bar customers, the congregation was made up of every extreme, hurting heart you can imagine. I fit right in.

I met Trey there. He was a victim of sexual abuse and had AIDS. He was unashamed to tell me that his life had been one train wreck after another. I felt loved and comforted by his open candidness. When I told him my story, he cried. He intimately knew the kind of pain I was going through, and for the first time, I didn't feel so alone or dirty. But how I felt about God was a different story.

As I dealt with being stalked and harassed, I felt myself start to lose the strength to keep going. I wanted to ask God for help, but where had God been all this time? Where had He been since I was twelve years old when my dad's anger outbursts first started? The idea of picturing God as a man or father was too much to bear. That left me nowhere. I felt like I had already failed at faith since God is supposed to be our heavenly Father. Forget it, I didn't need any more men hurting me.

When Trey heard me say these things, he suggested we pray together. He said he was going to bring a good friend who had also gone through a lot of trauma. I appreciated the gesture but didn't think it would do any good.

I expected them to lay hands on me and pray some lofty, impressive prayers. But instead they did sometime completely different. I'll never forget Trey's words: "We can pray a bunch of things for you, but why don't we ask God to speak to you since He knows exactly what you need to hear?" That meant the three of us were going to just sit together and listen. How hard could it be? Yet, I was terrified.

Even though it wasn't rational, I was afraid that God would hurt or abuse me. I didn't want to sit and ask Him to come. My breath sped up. I felt like I was going to have a panic attack. Was I this afraid of God? Was I this beyond repair?

Trey put his hand on my shoulder and said, "It's okay, Me Ra. God can take it, even if you can't picture Him as a man or father. All we can do is start from the honesty of where we are."

He and his friend closed their eyes and asked God to come. Not another word was said.

I struggled to close my eyes from this unexplainable panic that God may try to abuse me if I did. But a deep peace started to settle, and eventually I closed my eyes. With zero expectation, I let myself soak in that peaceful feeling. All of a sudden, I had a picture.

It came out of nowhere, almost like a movie playing in my mind. I was four or five years old and playing on a playground by myself when another little boy ran over and started playing with me. It felt like we laughed and played for hours. We went up and down on the teeter-totter, pumped our legs as hard as we could to go higher on the swings, went down the slide again and again, and spun in endless circles on the merry-go-round.

When the sun started to set, the little boy said he had to go home. As he walked away, I realized that I had never asked him what his name was. After all, kids don't need to know each other's name to play all afternoon. But I wanted to know his name. He turned around with a boyish grin and said, "My name's Jesus. I know you can't picture Me as a man. I know you're afraid to be around My Father. But I just want to be with you. I'll meet you here any time you want to play." And with that he ran off.

It was like a dam of tears broke, and I began to wail. A deep, buried pain of feeling abandoned by God was surfacing with the realization that He knew my name. He knew all my pain, and it wasn't too much for Him. People had prayed for me before, but this was the first time I felt like God knew my name. He knew the pain I was ashamed to admit. And He still cared. He didn't come with lectures about who He is, how He's my heavenly Father, how I should know better, with a finger wagging at me in condemnation. No. He came to me as a child. How did He know? How did He know this was what my heart needed? Even I didn't know.

For the next couple years, I met Jesus as a little boy. When the time was right, I started to get to know Him as the man and lover of my soul. I dove into the feminine side of God through the Holy Spirit. And eventually, I met the father heart of God. One step at a time. You can read more about my story in my first book, *Beauty Restored*, and how God pieced my shattered heart back together.

Throughout this season, I learned God is a gentleman who would rather sit with us in our pain, not even uttering a word, then have us feel alone. Most of all, I learned through my listening prayer time that He knew my name. The deep impact of hearing His voice, getting a picture from Him, changed everything.

I share this painful chapter in my life so that you know you're not alone. Many people believe it's impossible to hear God's voice. I think it's because they have years of noise blocking the air waves between them and God. The noise is made up of lies, pain, shame, disappointments, disillusionments, you name it—it's all taking up the radio waves between you and God. In fact, it would take an act of God to break through all the familiar lies you've been hearing most your life. That's what 4 Minutes is going to give you...an act of God.

Brian and I are convinced that the most powerful thing you can ever experience is that moment you realize God knows your name. Not anyone else's name, but your name. He knows your pain, your deepest hurts, your battered hopes, the things you struggle to forgive yourself for, and He loves you all the more. When you realize this and fully believe that God knows your name, your faith becomes unstoppable. Until that moment you start to doubt again and get knocked down by pain or grief. That's how you know it's time to do 4 Minutes again.

CHAPTER 3

A Shining Star in a Crystal Meth Lab

While I was nineteen and admitting myself to a locked psychiatric ward because my pain had become unbearable, Brian was going through his own pain. He has a "one in a million story" that most people struggle to believe. When Brian tells his story, there is rarely a dry eye in the room. As you read this, I hope I have done justice sharing it with you.

After high school, Brian left for college with high hopes and aspirations. Growing up, he was always the A+ student, member of the Debate Team, and dressed for success from head to toe. But when he got to college, his childhood pain started catching up with him. Wanting community and friendship, he joined a fraternity and earned the title for "Most Days Drunk." Within the first year, he was kicked out of the fraternity. From there, he started experimenting with drugs, and life took a fast, downward spiral.

By the time Brian was twenty years old, he had become mixed up with a biker gang. He lived with their chemist who made crystal meth. Sometimes Brian was up for weeks on speed. Brian is a living miracle. With all the hard drugs he did, there isn't any reason he should still be alive or shouldn't be half brain-dead. His life was like a mash up of *Breaking Bad* and *Sons of Anarchy*.

One night he was in a rage. He felt hurt, disrespected, and something needed to change. Summer was about to start, and he needed to decide about continuing to work with the chemist of the biker gang, listen to his parents, or do something related to his major. Not knowing what to do or who to listen to created a deep despair within him that fueled the rage. He got in a car and raced down the streets of Seattle. Thoughts of growing up with divorced parents, being sexually abused as a child, and doing things that he couldn't forgive himself for swirled in his head. He started screaming louder and louder, looking for a police car to ram into to end his pain.

All of a sudden, he had an open vision, like a picture in real time.

His car was charging toward a brick wall. Instead of hitting it, he was pulled out of the car through the windshield, set down, and confronted with a crossroads. To his right, everything was dark with a path full of even darker things. To his left, there was an unkept grass field with a soft dirt trail. At the head of that trail was a sign; the sign was a cross, and there was a man on the cross.

Brian said he knew who it was. He decided to get up in his face, feeling so much anger with this man on the cross. Brian looked him in the eyes and asked him, "Are you really who you say you are?"

He was somehow taken into the man's eyes and brain. Everything was clear. Over the years, Brian has told us stories from when he was doing drugs with the chemist for the biker gang, and he would see shadows move behind the chemist's eyes. But in this man's brain, everything was clear and calm. And Brian saw a word. The word was made out of stone. Brian knew it was his own name, but it wasn't the name *Brian*. Like in the Old Testament when God speaks creation into being, it was the word God used to speak Brian into being—the essence of all that he is.

When Brian saw his name, he was instantly taken out of the brain, out of the eyes, off the road, put back into his car, where he found himself screaming again in the driver's seat.

In complete shock, he pulled over to catch his breath and have a cigarette. He was trying to grasp what had just happened. Brian had just seen Jesus on the cross two thousand years ago, and Jesus was thinking about him. There were no doubts or regrets about who He was dying for.

Brian got out of the car and walked up the street to a park and got on his hands and knees. He told God that he would follow Him and tell people who he follows. I love how Brian said he expected fireworks after that, but there were none. So he smoked another cigarette and went back to his apartment that he shared with the chemist.

The next day, Brian walked to the music store to get guitar strings. He ran into a neighbor who told him the store was closed. Brian asked him where he was going, and the guy replied, "I'm going to church." To his neighbor's surprise, Brian said, "I'm going with you!" It was a Sunday night service.

Before he entered the church on 42nd and Brooklyn, Brian told God that if he felt His presence in that church, he would let everyone know he had become a follower of Jesus.

THE GUY IN THE WHITE T-SHIRT AND JEANS

That same night, I was back from the psychiatric ward trying to live a life of healing and wholeness. I sat in the back of the church with my friend when a young man walked in. He was sweating profusely. The pastor was already preaching, and this guy started walking up to the front of the church in the middle of the sermon. As he walked forward, he took off layer after layer of clothes until he was just in a white T-shirt and jeans, the sweat causing his T-shirt to stick to his chest and back.

I watched him fall on his knees in front of the pastor, lift his hands, and begin weeping. The whole church was silent. I think we were all in shock. We'd seen some wild things, but this was a first. I still remember the sound of his wailing. So much pain, so many tears.

The pastor asked a handful of guys to surround him, and they gathered around and started praying for Brian. But the only words they said were, "More Lord." We could all see God was at work, nothing more needed to be said. Brian must have cried for more than two hours.

During this time, he had a picture. There were clouds

that parted, and God's glory was like gold pouring over him like a waterfall. Then he heard a voice say, "I'm your Father, Brian. I'm your Father." He cried even harder when he heard these words. His heart asked, "How did You know? How did You know that's what I needed to hear? I didn't even know." He had always wondered if he was a product of his biology or his environment, being raised by his stepdad instead of his biological dad. Brian had a desperate need to know where he came from to know where he was going.

These are the questions so many of us are seeking answers to: Who am I? Who am I supposed to follow? What's my purpose?

God answered his question when He said, "I'm your Father." Paul adds to that in the New Testament when he writes, "The only accurate way to understand ourselves is by what God is and by what he does for us, not by what we are and what we do for him" (Romans 12:3 MSG).

After a couple hours Brian heard the worship band play the blues. He loved playing the harmonica and juice harp and thought, "I can go to a church where they play the blues."

When Brian got up to leave, the men who had been praying for him asked him if he was going to be okay. Did he need a place to stay for the night? He told them he was fine and left. Every time Brian tells this next part of the story, his face lights up. He said he felt like a shining star as he walked down the street that night! His whole body was clean, and he felt like light was beaming from every part of him.

He went back to his apartment, and the lights were on. But when Brian walked in, the chemist and the others there all covered their eyes, hid their faces, and said, "Where have you been?" Isn't that amazing? The lights were on, but Brian's spirit was shining so bright they had to cover their eyes!

It's a complete miracle that Brian never went through any drug withdrawals. All the crystal meth, speed, and cocaine he had done was over. But the drugs were only a symptom of the deeper pain that he then had to work through. The years to follow, especially our first five years of marriage, were filled with traumas too unspeakable to share. As hard as those years were, Brian never let go of that picture of seeing Jesus on the cross.

In Brian's darkest hour, God showed him that He knew his name.

CHAPTER 4

Single, Broke, and Hungry

Before Brian and I started dating, I hung out with a group of friends from church and college. We were all single, broke, and hungry for God. Now that you've read a little of our backstories, you can see why. Having come from extreme backgrounds of pain, we were desperate to hear God's voice.

How do you learn to hear God's voice? How do you know that what you hear is His voice and not your imagination? We had no idea. I had experienced it with the picture of Jesus as a little boy on the playground, but there was so much more to learn about God's voice.

Our group of friends decided to try an exercise. On Friday nights, we'd get together at someone's place. Each of us had a notepad. Setting the timer for five to ten minutes, we'd be still and ask God to speak to us about what to do that night or weekend. When the timer went off, we'd write down what we thought we heard, whether it was a certain word, picture, Bible verse, feeling, or sense of some kind, and then we'd share it with each other.

Here is the part we never expected. Every time, a handful of us would get the same thing. It was crazy! Like one of those heebie-jeebie moments. On top of that, what we heard during our listening prayer was random. It didn't connect to any previous conversations we'd been having with each other. There was no way for several of us to get the same detailed picture or word unless God was speaking to us.

Sometimes we felt like we should walk the streets of downtown Seattle or Capitol Hill because there was someone specific who needed prayer. We had no idea who the person was, but we decided to go and see if we could find them. We called these experiments "Adventures with God." Yep, this is what we were doing with our weekend nights in college.

Webster defines *adventures* as "an undertaking usually involving danger and unknown risks, an exciting or remarkable experience, and enterprise involving financial risk."

How did we find the person? I remember Pastor John Wimber once said you can always tell who is hurting if you look for the heads that are bowed. So we broke into small groups and walked the streets of Seattle, praying that God would lead us to the person who needed prayer, encouragement, and love.

The whole exercise felt risky—and, honestly, crazy. The

stranger was either going to be super offended, think we were crazy and tell us to go away, or open up to us. Could we handle the rejection and embarrassment? We decided that if one person felt loved, it was worth it. If the person wasn't open, we would keep moving forward. It also helped that we were in groups of three or four because we could lick our wounds of embarrassment together later.

What always got me back then (and still today), was how simple the word is. My ego wanted to hear some super, prophetic, earthshaking word. But I often heard things like, "Tell that person that God loves them." Really? Can't someone else tell them that? Why don't you tell me whether or not they should leave their job, if they're going to meet their spouse this year, or if their baby is going to be a boy or girl? I wanted to hear cool, sensational things like that.

Here's the deal...God knows what people need most. And it often lives in the simplicity of knowing God loves you. He knows your name. You are not forgotten or abandoned. When I spotted a specific person and felt butterflies in my stomach (usually my physical indicator that it was the right person), I felt terrified telling them those simple words.

The situation often went like this:

"Excuse me," I'd say with my heart beating at a rapid speed, "this is going to sound crazy. But I feel like I'm supposed to tell you something."

The person then looked at me as if I am crazy, assessing whether or not they should keep walking. But for some reason they didn't. They gave me a chance.

Gulp.

"I feel like I'm supposed to tell you that God loves you. Like really loves you. And He has not forgotten you."

Nine out of ten times there were tears, lots and lots of tears. Unbeknownst to me, these people needed to know that God loved them and had been asking God for a sign. The church they went to, whether they were Christians or not, was irrelevant. Their broken hearts were desperate for a sign that God still cared for them.

Through this vulnerable exercise, God started showing me the power of speaking a word in the Kairos moment. Merriam-Webster dictionary defines *Kairos* as "a time when conditions are right for the accomplishment of a crucial action: the opportune and decisive moment." Wikipedia explains *Kairos* as "an Ancient Greek word meaning the right, critical, or opportune moment."

There is a divine, critical, opportune moment for telling someone the exact thing their heart was asking God. A word, picture, or impression doesn't need to be flashy or fancy. The most important thing is that it needs to be in God's timing. And when it is, that person realizes God knows their name. He hasn't forgot them. He cares.

THE UNSPOKEN CRY OF HER HEART

Over the years, Brian and I have realized how complicated we can make prayer. We get caught into thinking we need to find the right formula of words to receive the breakthrough we need. But when someone is hurting and realizes God knows their name, nothing is more encouraging. Everything in their life changes.

Instead of jumping into praying for someone, we start by listening. This often throws people off because they expect you to say something out loud. There are no words to describe the look on their faces, an expression that shows they are deeply touched, when I ask if it's okay to start with us listening. I tell them what my friend Trey said to me when I was nineteen and broken: "I can pray a lot of things, but I'd rather listen and see what God wants to say." And the less you know about their circumstances, the better. That way, whatever you hear that is spot on with their current circumstances, you know is from God. It's faith building for everyone!

Most of the time, I don't remember the word I got for someone after I share it with them. Our family has prayed for countless people, and sometimes they will email years later about a word I had for them. For the life of me, I can't recall what I said. But their spirits never forgot it. Yet, there are a handful of listening prayer experiences that I have never forgotten, particularly one woman.

She came to our church one Sunday. I was still in college, single, and wanting to learn all I could about hearing God's voice. At the end of the service, the pastor invited anyone to come forward who needed prayer. I saw this woman come forward, bow her head, and wait on God. Butterflies were in my stomach (my physical feeling when I know God is asking me to do something), so I asked her if I could pray for her. I told her I was going to listen for her instead of saying words. She accepted the invitation but didn't say anything else.

As I stood with her in quiet, I had a clear picture of her sister dressed in the most beautiful white gown, dancing with Jesus. The picture was breathtaking. Jesus was twirling her around and making her sister laugh. Her sister was so alive, glowing, vibrant, happy, and at peace.

The butterflies in my stomach went crazy because I had no idea if I was in left field with this picture. We didn't talk at all about why she wanted prayer. I didn't even know if she had a sister. But that was the picture. So I started the same way I always do:

"Do you mind if I share a picture with you that I'm seeing? If it resonates with your heart, great. But if it doesn't, no worries. We'll just keep listening together."

She nodded.

As I told her the picture, her eyes filled with tears. Then she bent over, crying even more. And then a deep wailing came from her. Seeing her deep pain made me cry. I asked her if she had a sister. And she nodded yes. Still not sure why this picture would cause her to cry with such grief, I sat with her as the tears came and came and came. And I thanked God for the obvious healing that was happening, even though I had no idea what the backstory was.

At some point, a deep peace settled on the woman. The tears stopped. She blew her nose and thanked me. And then she took a deep breath. I remember it like it happened yesterday. She said that her youngest sister had committed suicide six months earlier. Her death had shattered her heart and world. Since her sister's death, she had been afraid to come back to church. She thought that if people knew what had happened, they would tell her that her sister was in hell. And she couldn't bear the pain of hearing that on top of losing her.

Now it was my turn to cry. Not knowing anything about her situation, God had shown me a picture of her sister dancing with Jesus. She was beautiful, vibrant, alive, and healed. Regardless of anyone's theology, there is no way I could have imagined that picture without knowing her situation. God was showing this woman in the most powerful, intimate, gentle way that He knew her name. He knew her sister's name. And He loved them both deeply.

God is so good. Retelling the story makes me cry as I write it. It was a moment almost thirty years ago that I will never forget. It was such a simple picture that didn't mean anything to me, and yet it was the exact Kairos word her heart needed most.

Doing 4 Minutes for other people is about letting go of needing to know the meaning behind what you got. Brian and I often don't know the meaning. God asks us to be obedient and share it anyways—even though it doesn't make any sense to us. That's part of the faith walk, the requirement in listening for other people. You're willing to first humble yourself by not needing to have all the answers. All that matters is whether it means something to the person receiving it.

The big question is this: Are you willing to look like a fool? There have been a handful of times in the last thirty years when the person looked at me like I was crazy and walked away. A handful is nothing compared to all the other times the person gave me a chance. But those handful of times can make you feel foolish. That's why you need a spiritual community to grow with. If you're single, it can be a few good friends who want to risk looking foolish and hearing from God. You never know what kind of impact you'll have on someone's life just when they need it.

THE SIMPLEST WORD IS OFTEN THE MOST POWERFUL

Once I was speaking at a women's event at a church in Dallas, Texas. At the end of my talk, I had everyone take some time to be still together. To my left was a lady with long, dark brown hair. I never really see visible things on people, but this night I did. It was like she had a sign on her forehead that said the word *life*.

Life.

That's a pretty simple word, right? Even though this was after years of practicing how to hear from God and doing this 4 Minute listening time with Brian and my kids, I still had a moment of doubt. I still felt like the word *life* was too simple. Would it do any good to even tell her? I decided to tell her because I knew what would happen if I didn't.

Over the years, God has shown me again and again that He won't give me another picture or word until I share the last one. Sometimes I'm not supposed to share the word right away, and I will sit on it for weeks, even months. Other times, I have those butterflies and know I'm supposed to share it right away. If I don't, I won't get anything in our 4 Minutes until I do.

I don't feel like God is punishing me. I feel like He's saying He can't fill my mailbox again until I empty what's already in there.

I lifted the mic up and got the lady's attention. Well, I got everyone's attention because I was speaking into a mic. I told her that I saw the word *life* written across her forehead. And then more words came to me. The mailbox was empty, and God was already filling it back up in real time. I sensed that her legacy was going to be life and not death. That's it. No one in the audience oohed or awed. Instead, it was a sea of confused faces, as if everybody was saying "That's it?"

Then she started crying. And her crying went deeper into wailing.

As I stood on the stage with the woman wailing, I remembered going to my first Christian youth conference in Anaheim, California, at nineteen. Pastor John Wimber, founder of the Vineyard Christian Fellowship, looked like Santa Claus. With a white beard and big belly, he sat at the front of the church. Three thousand teenagers were there. He said that he was going to invite God to come and spend time with us and not to be afraid of what it looks like when God shows up. He said some of us may cry, others laugh, others be completely still. God was trustworthy, and He would give each of us what we came for.

So I told everyone that God was in this place, bringing healing, and not to be afraid. I think it's powerful when the church can hold a sacred, safe space for the brokenhearted. This wasn't a Sunday morning; this was a special evening service for the women. It felt like the perfect time and space for all of us to hold this space for her.

When the evening was over, the lady found me. With tears in her eyes, she said that she arrived late. She had been sitting in the church parking lot contemplating suicide that night. Should she come in or should she just end it all? That was the question she'd been asking.

She made a deal with God and told Him she'd come to one more service and not kill herself if He gave her a sign that her life was worth living. That He had life for her. Even years later, I cry sharing this story with you. I had almost dismissed the word *life* because it seemed too simple to me. I almost didn't share it with her because I didn't want to look and feel foolish in front of the audience. But God knew exactly what she needed to hear. Life.

These stories are an example of the amazing gifts we can give to people. All it takes is 4 Minutes. But I didn't start with standing on a stage in front of a thousand women. I started with my own pain of not being able to see God as a man or father and meeting the young boy named Jesus by surprise. And then I practiced with college friends I trusted and felt safe with. Eventually, Brian brought new meaning to the 4 Minutes after we were married.

Part 2

Creating a Marriage and Family Culture

CHAPTER 5

All I Wanted Was to Pray with My Husband

Before I got married, I had lofty visions of my husband and I someday praying together by our bedside. Both of our hands folded, heads bowed, reverently seeking God's face and voice.

And then I met my husband.

For starters, Brian never closes his eyes when he prays. Ever. In the early years of our marriage, we would be going through something super stressful. And one of us would suggest praying together. Well, even though we started with good intentions, we would be arguing within a couple of minutes.

I was frustrated because Brian was looking all around the room instead of closing his eyes and focusing on praying. He said, "God doesn't need me to close my eyes."

"Are you even praying?" I'd ask with a not so subtle tone of judgment in my voice.

He'd answer, "How would you know if *your* eyes are closed?"

Touché.

Our first five years of marriage was full of trauma. I never want to go back to those early years, but I'm also thankful for them because of how much we learned. Praying together was one of the biggest gifts we received from that difficult season.

After several failed attempts of praying together, Brian finally suggested, "Why don't we set the timer for four minutes and both shut up!"

He was stressed that I would never stop praying. I inherited my Korean grandmother's gift of intercession and serious stamina for prayer. Brian's ADHD couldn't handle long-winded prayer times. Setting the timer for four minutes to listen seemed like a fair middle ground.

I asked him why it was four minutes and not five or ten? He said that ten was a long time to sit quietly. We could always add more minutes if four wasn't long enough. Five minutes felt like it could get rounded up to fifteen. But how can you say no to four minutes? He'd counter, "I mean, who doesn't have four minutes in their day to just stop and listen? And if you say you don't, really? You really don't have four minutes?"

I loved him for that answer. Brian knows my personality. I am a recovering Type A, Enneagram #1 (aka Perfectionist), and ENFJ, whatever that means. I love order, structure, a plan, and I really struggle when those things fall apart.

Brian is a complete optimist. He's an Enneagram #7 (aka the Life of the Party). He thrives on being spontaneous, love adventure, and believes it's all going to work out. I have this feeling that he could see into our future and knew I would have moments of such stress because my plan was being turned upside down. But did I have four minutes? How could I say no to four minutes?

So, we did it. We started with setting the timer for four minutes, listening like we did in our early twenties when we were single and desperate to hear God's voice. We were desperate again, except now we were married. There were big decisions to make, like buying our first home or continuing to invest our savings into marriage counseling. Both of us came from a lot of trauma and knew we needed all the help we could get. I'll never forget doing 4 Minutes on that decision.

When the timer went off, Brian said he had a picture of building our home through Christian marriage counseling. Even though it was hard to wait on buying a house (especially when all of our friends were doing it), he said he felt like we were building a home instead by staying committed to work through the hard things. Instead of buying our first home, we were building our house on the rock to survive the rains.

POWER OF AGREEMENT

Brian grew up with a mom who burned her bra and ironed her hair during the Feminist Movement in the '60s and

'70s. Women were fighting for their voice to be heard and to be treated with respect in the home, workplace, and society. He also grew up going to church off and on and hearing sermons based on Ephesians 5 where Paul writes, "Wives, submit yourselves to your own husbands as you do to the Lord" (v. 22). I grew up with an authoritative, traditional Korean father who expected obedience and submission. But that same chapter goes on to say, "Husbands, love your wives, just as Christ loved the church and gave himself up for her...husbands ought to love their own wives as their own bodies. He who loves his wife loves himself" (vv. 25, 28).

In our marriage, we interrupted those verses not as an excuse for husbands flexing authority but to cultivate a marriage built on mutual respect. We made a commitment to always be in agreement when facing a decision where the other spouse might be left with negative feelings.

For example, Brian wanted to buy a new car, but it made me feel stressed because I didn't feel like we had the money at the time. I also thought we were saving for a vacation. Brian felt like it was more of a risk not to get a new car because he was worried our current car was going to break down. Both of us had valid points. Which direction do you go?

If we weren't able to reach an agreement through talking it out, where we both felt peace with the decision, we would do 4 Minutes. If we didn't have an answer or peace after the 4 Minutes, we'd do it again and again until we did. Choosing to wait for peace versus jeopardizing our unity is always more valuable.

Let me say that again in another way. *Unity in a marriage is more important than being right.* Your marriage and family can't survive if you're divided.

Our hunger for peace and unity in our home increased so that we wanted all our decisions to be in alignment with the Holy Spirit. What we learned from this is that even when we were in unity, we still needed to take time and do 4 Minutes. We wanted to give God an opportunity to speak to us, even when we thought we didn't need to hear His voice.

Sometimes God would change one of our minds or hearts to the other person's opinion. And sometimes God would reveal a new path that neither of us had considered. Going back to the car example—we did 4 Minutes and had a new idea to buy a used car that would save us money but also be much more dependable than the one we owned. It might seem obvious that we could have figured this out without doing 4 Minutes. But when emotions are running high, it's hard to be open to the other person's point of view.

If I felt like our savings or family vacation was being threatened, I couldn't hear another point of view. If the car would have broken down, Brian would have felt like he'd failed as a husband and dad who protects his family and makes sure they're safe. This is the magic of 4 Minutes. As those minutes go by, God calms down powerful emotions so we can be a team again.

ALTARS TO ANCHOR US

Sometimes we would do the 4 Minutes, come to a place of agreement, and move forward, only to run into more challenges. Did we hear wrong? Doing the 4 Minutes together is like building an altar, the way people did in ancient times. It becomes this tangible point in your timeline when you can look back and encourage each other that God brought you to this point. It's His responsibility to take care of you as you move forward.

When the Israelites crossed the Jordan, they built an altar in remembrance of God being with them. After Jacob ran away, he had a dream of angels ascending and descending. The next morning, he built an altar to signify that this is where he'd heard from God. These stone altars were spiritual mile markers in their faith, pointing to the moment God spoke to their hearts.

If Brian and I are struggling with knowing what to do about a challenge we're facing with family, business, finances, etc., we do 4 Minutes. And we do it again and again until we feel peace about which direction to go. Whatever we hear, we write it all down. The 4 Minutes is a spiritual mile marker that we can look back on when fear and doubt start to creep in. It's a tangible, physical moment that we could point back to for reassurance.

RENEWING YOUR MIND FIRST

Brian added one more thing to this practice of listening prayer. He started with reading Joshua 1 from *The Message* translation. Every time we got to the words, "Strength! Courage!" he insisted that we throw a fist in the air as if we were going to war, like a battle cry. Our teenagers have come to love this. If Dad didn't feel like you meant it, he'd read it all over again!

But Brian was on to something. Living a life that willingly chooses to step into the unknown, building an impossible dream, take guts. You have to approach it like a warrior, knowing you're going to battle fear, doubt, and anxiety along the way! Brian felt like we needed to rile our spirits before we set the timer for four minutes.

We've been reading this same passage out loud for more than twenty years. Our kids literally know it by heart. Sometimes they start randomly reciting it to us, just to make us laugh. What's crazy is that depending on what we're facing, a different line or phrase sticks out to me every single time.

Joshua 1 gives us this deep comfort that God is for us, not against us. There have been seasons when I have felt so discouraged that I wept as Brian read the verses. My shout of "Strength! Courage!" was barely audible. There have been other seasons when I felt so full of faith that I couldn't sit as he read the verses, wanting to march right out of the living room. What I love most is the idea of starting with truth before you set your timer for four minutes.

Reminding yourself of who God is, that He is for you and not against you, and that He is with you every step you take, are powerful truths to recall. Let's call it building your faith and resetting your mind, heart, and spirit as you set the timer for four minutes to hear God's voice. I've broken down the part we read line by line, so you can see the power in every piece of this passage. It was true for Joshua thousands of years ago, and it's true for us today. Remember to throw your fist in the air like a warrior when you get to the "Strength! Courage!" parts.

It's all yours.
All your life, no one will be able to hold out against you.
In the same way I was with Moses, I'll be with you.
I won't give up on you; I won't leave you.
Strength! Courage!

You are going to lead this people to inherit the land that I promised to give their ancestors.

Give it everything you have, heart and soul.

Make sure you carry out The Revelation that Moses commanded you, every bit of it.

Don't get off track, either left or right,

so as to make sure you get to where you're going.

And don't for a minute let this Book of The Revelation be out of mind.

Ponder and meditate on it day and night,

making sure you practice everything written in it.

Then you'll get where you're going; then you'll succeed.

Haven't I commanded you?

Strength! Courage!

Don't be timid; don't get discouraged.

God, your God, is with you every step you take.

(Joshua 1 MSG)

CHAPTER 6

Little Detective Notebooks

B rian and I have always believed the most important gift
you can give your kids is to teach them how to hear
God's voice. If they can hear and discern God's voice
from all the other noise in this world, they will be fine.

Blaze was four and Pascaline was seven when we first
started teaching them 4 Minutes. But we didn't start with four
minutes. They were little kids with short attention spans. And
this was a practice we wanted to cultivate in them throughout
their childhood, so we started with thirty seconds. We could all
do thirty seconds, no matter how many wiggles the kids had.

Those early days were so funny. Little Blazey would be jumping on the coach until the moment Brian started the timer. He'd take one last jump, land flat on his bottom, and throw his head back, squeezing his eyes shut, trying with all his might to be quiet for thirty seconds.

Pascaline took everything much more seriously. After all, she wasn't four. She was seven. In perfect posture, she would fold her hands and sit at the edge of her chair. With her chin tilted upward and eyes closed, she was the epitome of reverence.

When the timer went off, and we asked the kids if they saw a picture or word or felt a sense of anything. For the first several times, they both shook their heads no. Blaze went back to jumping on the couch, and Pascaline's perfect posture fell into a defeated slouch. "Mama, even if I do hear something, how do I know it's God voice and not my imagination?"

Such a great question.

Isn't that what we all wonder? How do we know we're hearing God's voice versus indigestion from dinner the night before? Learning to discern God's voice from all the distractions, fears, and doubts we're bombarded by takes practice. Little detective notebooks are perfect for this part of the journey!

The next time we got together for 4 Minutes, I had detective notebooks for each of us. We told the kids that hearing from the Lord is often like listening for clues to solve a puzzle. Sometimes God gives each of us our own piece in the puzzle, and when we put them together the picture or word makes sense. But we also need to grow in our faith and confidence that God really wants to and is speaking to us.

I looked at Pascaline and said, "I'm going to ask God to

give me the exact same word or picture that He gives you. That way you know it's God because there's no other way that could happen."

Her eyes got wide. That didn't even seem possible to her. But I knew from our time of practicing listening prayer with friends in our twenties that God was more than able. And not only is God able, but He *loves* this kind of thing! His kids making time to learn how to hear His voice…what could delight Him more?

We set the timer again for thirty seconds. Blaze fell on the couch and squeezed his eyes shut. Pascaline leaned forward, really trying to listen. When the timer went off, we each wrote down what we got. Since Blaze was only four, he drew a picture. Pascaline wrote a couple words down. To her surprise, I had written down the same exact thing. For the next couple years, almost every time we did 4 Minutes, Pascaline and I had the same thing. It was powerful in building her faith and continually strengthening mine.

DIFFERENT WAYS GOD SPEAKS

Whether you have young children or older kids, this is a great exercise to start with them. Buy multicolored notebooks at the grocery store—the ones that cost less than a dollar each. Everybody gets their own. And tell your kids that you're not only going to ask God to speak during your listening time but you're also going to ask Him to share the same thing with some of you. This will build your faith and your kids' faith more than you could ever imagine!

In the beginning, my desire was simple. I prayed for a

single word, and I prayed that Pascaline would get the same word. It didn't matter yet that we understood the purpose of the word. You have to learn to hear before you can learn to understand what you're hearing.

Ask God for this simple gift. Ask Him to give you and your spouse the same word. Let go of needing to understand what the word means. Ask Him to give you and your kids the same word. Maybe the word is *peace*, *hope*, or *joy*. They're all simple words, but the cool, goosebumps part is when you and your kid get the same word without even asking for it!

After this had happened with Pascaline several times, I started having her pay attention to how her body physically felt when she'd get a word, picture, or verse. I wanted her to look for signs that her physical body was giving her outside of what she was sensing. Was there a consistent feeling in her tummy that seemed to happen when she got a word? Paying attention to these kinds of details helps us discern when God is speaking versus our imagination.

Even if the kids didn't get anything, they were still expected to sit and listen to what their dad and I got. Part of the listening practice is sharing what you sensed with close friends or family and then writing it down. Sometimes the pictures, words, and Bible verses make sense right away. Other times, they don't make any sense at all. That's why we love to write it all down. We were also casting vision for the kids on what it looked like to hear from the Lord, and how each of us hears in a different way.

The kids started noticing how Dad's pictures and words are often abstract with lots of different pieces to them. And they're often connected to something he sees in the living room at the moment. (Remember, Brian never closes his eyes when he prays!) Mom's pictures and words are often more direct. The family nicknamed me "Mailbox" because I would get the same words and pictures that Pascaline got and then another few. I loved watching their faces light up, excited to hear what God had spoken to us. This joy and delight are what Brian and I wanted to cultivate in their hearts: a desire, excitement, and expectation to hear God's voice.

After a while, our family started writing everything down in a prayer journal. Get your family your own prayer journal. Pick a blank book with a great cover that inspires you instead of making use of an empty journal around the house. These pages are going to hold your family's most sacred, adventure-filled stories. The risks you learned to take with God, the little ways you heard His voice, and the mysteries to still unravel will all live in these pages.

Over the last twelve years, our family has filled up three of those journals with endless pictures, words, and Bible verses. We're currently halfway through our fourth book. If there was a fire in our home, and I could only grab one thing, I would grab these four journals. They are the telling of our family's history, of all the things God has shared with us over the years, and the behind-the-scene stories to where we got the courage to take the adventures we've had. Every adventure we've ever taken, every career decision we've ever made, every family decision started with 4 Minutes and is found in those pages. It's not only our history of learning to hear God's voice together and for each other but it's also our testimonies of all the mysterious ways God has revealed Himself.

CHAPTER 7

God Loves Legos Too

I had it all wrong.

When Blaze was five years old, he went through a season where his hand would shoot up every time the timer went off. And every time, he had the same picture. He saw us buying boxes of Legos for different kids and shipping them to their families.

I'd smile and tell Blaze that was super sweet, but we weren't going to buy Legos every week for kids. Besides, didn't he know Legos were expensive? And God doesn't play with Legos, right?

Blaze's life revolved around building Legos with his dad. I assumed that's why he kept getting this same picture. But this went on and on. The next time the timer went off, his hand would shoot up again. His reoccurring picture went from cute to exhausting. I started challenging him to listen for something different. But it never worked. His picture was always the same: buying Legos for another family.

One morning while I was walking the dog, the Lord spoke to me. I will never forget it. My walk led me to a certain bluff in the neighborhood that overlooked the Puget Sound waters. I heard God speak to my heart, "If Blaze thinks it is too crazy for Me to tell him to buy Legos for other kids, how is he going to believe it's My voice when he's older and I share even more out-of-the-box words and pictures with him?" My whole spirit went still. I heard the holy rebuke loud and clear.

Why couldn't God tell Blaze to buy Legos for other kids? In trying to teach Blaze to hear God's voice, I was the one missing it. I went right home and asked my five-year-old son to forgive me. And not only that, I told him we were going to Target that day to buy all those Legos and ship them off to other kids. And we did!

After that, something shifted in little Blazey. He was thrilled that I believed he was hearing from the Lord. And he was super excited to ship Legos for all the random kids he'd had pictures of. When your kids are little, finances always seem tight. Buying a ton of Legos wasn't in our budget, but I knew I had heard God's rebuke on that bluff. I had to take this risk, no matter how much money it cost.

The following week, Brian and I were going through a ton of stress with work. Lies had been circulating about my character within the photography industry. I was feeling vulnerable, attacked, and helpless. My head and heart were spinning, so Brian asked the kids to join us for 4 Minutes.

Sure enough, when the timer went off Blaze's hand shot straight up.

I took a deep breath and willed myself to have a good attitude about his picture of Legos. After buying all those Legos and shipping them off, he was probably wanting to do it again. But my patience and wallet couldn't afford it. I braced myself and asked Blazey to share his picture.

I will never forget what my five-year-old said.

He scooted his little body off the couch and stood up. "Mama, I had a picture of you!"

"Of me?"

"Yes! You were walking across a wooden bridge. Sharks were jumping out of the water trying to bite your feet. You were scared, Mama. You didn't think you were going to make it to the other side. Every time you took a step, a big shark ate that step. And just when you thought you'd fall in the water and be eaten by sharks, God's hands reached down from heaven and held you and took you to the other side."

I sat there crying. Over a decade later, I'm crying again as I write this because I can remember that moment like it was yesterday. I can remember his chubby, little hands acting out God's hands, reaching down to hold me and lead me to the other side. Blaze had no idea what we were going through with work, but God knew. And because I had acted on believing Blaze about all his pictures of Legos, it had freed him up to hear even more.

This was the beginning of Blaze hearing from the Lord. In fact, I don't remember him getting many more pictures of Legos after that. But he has since had endless pictures for backpackers sitting alone in a bar in Thailand, pastors going through a dark time, Muslims in Egypt. And he shares his words, pictures, and senses with solid confidence because he knows God speaks to him. He's been hearing His voice since he was five years old.

CHAPTER 8

New Year's Day Traditions

After a couple years, the kids started developing more and more stamina for doing 4 Minutes versus thirty seconds. It's a listening practice that must be practiced. The more you practice, the easier it gets. Although the kids still often joke that thirty seconds should be enough too.

Growing up, I had a few different Korean New Year's traditions in our family that I now cherish as an adult. Brian and I wanted our family of four to have our own New Year's tradition, and so we started doing 4 Minutes for each other on New Year's Day.

The focus is listening for what God has in the coming year. We start by reviewing the words we had the year before and how those words came to pass or still feel like mysteries. Each person gets their own turn. The kids often joke that it should be called "Four Hours," because by the time we're done reading what we wrote last year, talking about it, doing a new 4 Minutes for the coming year, and then sharing all of that and writing it down, each person can take up to an hour. We don't mean for that to happen, but the kids will assure you that it happens every year.

What could be a better way to start the year then listening for four minutes about what God had for each person in the family? What I didn't realize is how powerful it would be for building our relationships with each other.

I'll never forget the year Blaze said he had a picture of Pascaline making some really great friends in the coming year. He's three years younger than his big sister. Whether or not he realized that she was struggling with friendships didn't matter. He spoke life into his sister's future, and she received it.

One year I had a word that God loved Blaze's sense of humor. The word made my heart smile. It was so sweet. Blaze was quiet as a little boy, and this was a word that was calling him out of the shadows. Ten years later, I think we'd all agree that he is one of the funniest people in our family. He makes all of us laugh every day.

A TRADITION YOU CAN DO ON YOUR OWN

Another tradition that I have done for years is doing 4 Minutes by myself, listening for my "Word of the Year." I'll do

4 Minutes a handful of times in December and January, pressing in for that single word that is going to be my focus for the next twelve months.

After I do 4 Minutes, I'll spend time journaling on different words that I think it might be. One year the word that came to me was *soak*. At first glance that word didn't make any sense because I hate baths. That was the first thing that *soak* made me think of. I listened for another word, journaled, but soak kept coming back to me. I finally decided to ask Brian what he thought. His response made me cry.

It was our last full year before Pascaline was headed to college. He felt like God was giving me permission to spend the year soaking her up. When I came home from a speaking engagement and had the option to start laundry or go for a walk with her, he looked at me and smiled. "This year, be confident that God is saying take the walk with her. Soak her up." And so I did. I had the word engraved on a necklace to remind me every day I looked in the mirror. Every other Sunday afternoon, Pascaline and I did Starbucks trips where we'd bring our laptops and work on the novels we were both writing. We took long walks. If my mind ever started to second-guess what to spend my time on, all I had to do was feel my necklace and remember that God had given me my word for the year.

I love speaking on the power of choosing a "Word for the Year." There is something powerful about being intentional and choosing a single word. Throughout the coming months that word will be like a teacher, giving us insight into the deeper meanings of the word. It will often wave to us among a sea of doubt and fear, reminding us we are not alone. That single word is still pushing through the year with us.

In 2020, my word was *thankful*. Pascaline had moved out

and gone to college. I needed a word that would remind me to reflect on all the wonderful adventures and time we shared as a family. I had no idea that COVID-19 was around the corner, and it would ultimately bring her back home to do school online.

The word *thankful* took on new meaning. It went from being a comfort to my grief as a mom to becoming a sharp, powerful sword as anxiety, fear, and doubt consumed the world with an unprecedented pandemic. Starting my prayer time each morning with thankfulness has been an anchor to my soul during the pandemic.

Whether you're single, married, or have a family, I encourage you to do 4 Minutes for your "Word for the Year." Journal about the word, ask it to teach you the depths of its meaning, and let it walk alongside you, giving you strength as you face the unknown.

ONE MORE 4 MINUTES

After everyone has gone, and we've shared our "Word for the Year," we really push the kids! We have them do one more 4 Minutes for the family as a whole. What does God have for our family this year? For the most part, the words are often simple and broad. It's still fun to listen.

But then one year, everything changed. It was the first and only year we all got the same word.

The word was *GO!*

PART 3

Stepping into the Unknown

CHAPTER 9

What If I Emailed Egypt?

Before we're done on New Year's Day, we do one more 4 Minutes. This is when the kids collapse on the couch because they don't know if they can take any more. Brian and I smile at each other because we love making our kids suffer. (I write that with a big smile.) The last 4 Minutes is a general one for our family as a unit. The question we're holding before God is, "What do you have for our family this coming year?"

One year we all had the same word. It had never happened

before and hasn't happened since. You can imagine the goosebumps we got when we realized it the word was *go*!

Even though each of us had the word *go*, we each had different pictures that went with the word. One of the kids had a picture of the globe spinning, and they stopped it with their finger on the Middle East. The other one had a picture of us riding camels with the pyramids in the background. Brian had a picture of himself opening up a map of the world and pointing to Egypt. I had a picture of us packing up and heading out. We were all blown away. No one had been talking or thinking about Egypt. Were we supposed to go to Egypt?

Egypt. I was so excited! The idea sounded amazing! Who doesn't want to see the pyramids? And the fact that we all had the word *go* was incredible! Brian and I assumed this new year was going to hold more travel than we'd ever done before. Instead, it was the first year in several years that we didn't travel anywhere.

We also didn't have cable TV. Instead, we used Apple TV or Netflix. Keeping up with world news had to be intentional on our part since we weren't seeing it on TV every day. I remember going to my parents' home for dinner and seeing mass rioting in the streets of Cairo. I had no idea that the people of Egypt were all over the news with their country's revolution for a democracy. As a mom, I stepped back and thought, "There's no way God wants our family to go to Egypt when the news is showing endless footage of rioting and fires in the streets."

Yet, every time we did our 4 Minutes as a family, Egypt came up again and again. This happened for several months until Brian and I finally decided we needed to look into the possibility of going. Our first step was to talk with people who had boots on the ground. A friend of a friend knew people in the CIA who were in Egypt. We asked them to see if things were as bad as the US news was showing. After years of traveling to Thailand, we had witnessed how the US news often exaggerates the stories of other countries and their stability.

I remember us being in the Bangkok airport, having just arrived in Thailand. My mom called to see if we were all okay. The US news was reporting a major bombing. But we were there, and there wasn't any bombing. However, this news alone tanked Thailand's tourism economy for several months. Was Egypt really this bad or was the US news just making it look that way?

Several sources from Cairo came back and said that things weren't that bad at all. The exaggerated coverage of the US news had all but destroyed their tourism, which is more than 50 percent of the country's economy. When Brian and I heard this, our hearts were heavy. A determination started to build in us. We wanted to take our expertise of photography and filming to Egypt and tell the world another story.

At the time I was writing a weekly column for Disney's largest parent website. With this vision in mind, I asked them if I could write a series of articles about our family's time in Egypt. This would be an incredible distribution channel. They said yes! Now we had to figure out how to get there, where to go, and how to pay for it all.

We looked at our funds. We had enough money to fly us to Egypt but not enough to pay for us to stay more than a few days. Brian and I brainstormed a bunch of ways we could make money to go as a family, but nothing gave us peace. The constant brainstorming process was so mentally exhausting that one night I said to the kids, "What if I just emailed Egypt?"

Their big brown eyes lit up, and they said, "Sure, Mom! That's a great idea! Yeah! Email Egypt!"

So that's what I did, folks! I emailed Egypt. How do you email a country? I literally sat in front of my computer and came up with every kind of Egypt email address I could think of like tourism@egypt.com or info@travelegypt.com. Those have to land in Egypt, right? I looked up tourism companies who specialized in Egypt. I sent the same email. I said that my husband and I were professional photographers and videographers. We saw the news of Egypt's revolution and the turmoil that the country was going through. But we also heard that it was safe to travel to Egypt, even as a family. We wanted to bring our two kids and capture a different story than what the news was telling. And Disney would help us share that story through their parenting website. All in all, I sent forty of these emails out.

The next morning, I almost forgot to check my inbox. One email had come back. It was a tourism company that had started in Egypt years ago. The email said that if we could cover the airfare, they would take care of everything else for a month of travel in Egypt! They loved that we had the expertise to tell a different story, and they wanted our family and the world to see that Egypt was still an amazing country and culture to experience. Two months later, our family was packed and flying to Cairo.

We had a layover in Germany, and Brian and I will never forget the boarding process. The flight called for the first fifteen rows to board. Only the Egyptian men got up. All the women and children stayed behind. They boarded at the end, after the men were all seated. That was our first tip headed to a foreign country that was unlike any we'd ever experienced.

It was dark when we arrived. Tom, one of our guides for the next month, was there to great us with the kindest smile. As we drove along the freeway, I noticed that one side of the freeway was lit with streetlamps, stores, and markets. But the other side of the freeway was pitch dark. Tom explained that the left side was the City of Dead. Egyptians had been burying their dead there for years, but it wasn't a cemetery. It was a literal city with stores, homes, and streets reserved for the dead.

The kids have joked for years that Brian and I won't let them spend the night at a friend's home, but we'll fly them into a country that is fighting for a revolution. When we arrived in Egypt, they were celebrating the two-year anniversary of their revolution. Mohamed Morsi had been elected as president of Egypt with hope that he would lead the country to a new place of democracy. But he turned out to be a puppet for the Muslim Brotherhood regime, and the country was suffering more than ever.

To get gas, our driver had to get in line at 3 a.m. The pyramids that average nearly fifteen million tourists a year were empty. The world was terrified of traveling to Egypt. The upside is that it made our job much easier. Without crowds of tourists, we were able to photograph and film the culture and country.

On our first morning, we were introduced to our Egyptologist guide named Ben. He had the biggest smile and loudest laugh. His passion for his country, people, and history was contagious. After breakfast, he took us on a walking tour through the streets of Cairo, teaching us about the city's many wonders. We came to intersections where one corner had a Jewish synagogue, the other corner had a Coptic Christian church, and the third corner had a Muslim mosque. "See!" he'd say with a bright face. "All the religions in one place, living together in peace for years. What you see on the news is not the true Egypt. This is Egypt."

Ben asked if he could spend extra time with our kids, teaching them the history of his religion and their politics. He said the children are our future. "If they understand where my family has come from. They'll help others understand too." Brian and I loved it all. Ben knew we were Christians, but he could also tell that we wanted our kids to respect every faith and culture, especially the ones most foreign to us.

We walked into the tombs in the Valley of the Kings where the hieroglyphics looked as if they had just been painted because the paint colors were still so vibrant after thousands of years. Without any rain or moisture in the air, the tombs were preserved beyond belief. Ben pointed to the top of the hieroglyphics and read the story of the Pharaoh's life. It was mesmerizing!

As phenomenal as our trip was, I couldn't help but feel discouraged. The tour company had helped us set up a handful of interviews for me to have with different Egyptian woman. One by one, they were all cancelled. Ben was also discouraged. He told us how Egypt had always been the most liberal country in the Middle East. His own mom was a famous professor. He said that three years ago, none of the women covered their heads. But their country was under a cultural attack from the Muslim Brotherhood regime, and now all women covered their heads. He felt like his country was going backward, and he was desperate to fight against it. The cancelled interviews broke his heart even more.

When you travel with someone for a month, sailing down the Nile River, dancing along the riverbanks together with

Nubians, riding camels to ruins, and then camping in the White Desert in the Valley of the Whales, you learn a lot about each other. Ben became more than an Egyptologist Guide; he became our friend.

Throughout our whole month, I kept asking God if we were doing enough. With the cancelled interviews, I often felt like I was failing. We stayed at the Marriott hotel for a couple nights along the Red Sea in Sharm El Sheikh. My daughter and I walked out to the pool in our bathing suits, thinking it was acceptable because it was the Marriott. Women were draped in black burqas, covered from head to toe and playing with their kids in the swimming pool. I looked at my bathing suit revealing all my limbs and felt every eye on me. I quickly covered myself.

Three Egyptian women in burqas were talking poolside. We only had a few days left before we had to fly home, and I still hadn't been able to interview any women. So I decided to be bold and approach them. I asked them if I could ask them a few questions about their country and faith.

The women looked over at a man, one of their husbands, who was bald with a long beard.

He asked me to repeat my question to him. And then he had a handful of questions for me. Why was I interested? What was I going to do with the information they shared? Once he was satisfied with my answers and motives, he nodded to the women. I assumed he was going to translate, but he got up and walked away. One of the women leaned forward and in perfect English asked me what my first question was.

It was a fascinating twenty-minute conversation of her telling me that the burqas gave her freedom by helping her feel safe. She never had to worry about giving men the wrong impression because she was fully covered. At home, she took it off with her husband and children. My heart walked away heavy. Years later, I'm still processing our conversation.

Our last night with Ben finally came. We had shared our hearts with each other over the last month. I knew he would trust our motives when I asked him if our family could pray for him before we said good-bye. He said yes, and we invited him back to our hotel room.

I told him that our family loved to do a listening type of prayer. We set the timer for four minutes and just listen to what God wants to say to the person. Sometimes we get a single word, a picture, or a Bible verse. Would he be okay if we set the timer together and listened for him? He looked at us with his genuine warm smile and nodded yes.

There is something so powerful when you sit for four minutes with the intent of listening for one person. Even if no one hears or senses anything in that four minutes, lives are changed because the Holy Spirit is there and moving in mysterious ways. This night, when the timer went off and we opened our eyes, Ben was wiping tears from his eyes. None of us had shared anything, but God was already moving on his heart.

Each of us had a picture for him. I don't remember what Brian and I had, but we wrote it all down. However, I do remember what the kids saw. Blaze was only ten years old at the time. Whenever a child shares what they feel like God has shown them, it breaks past all the walls that surround someone's heart. The picture or words are so pure, your heart can't help but receive them.

Blaze had a picture of Ben walking through Egypt with

his daughter on his shoulders. He said that she was able to see past all the chaos and fighting because of how high her dad lifted her up. And then Blaze told Ben in a ten-year-old version that he didn't have to be afraid for his daughter. She was going to be okay because she had her dad.

Pascaline often gets pictures with immense detail. A lot of the time she doesn't understand what she's seeing. This was one of those times. She started by saying she had a picture of Mr. Ben walking down a dark tunnel. There was a light at the end of the tunnel and above his head was a symbol. She had never seen this symbol before and didn't know what it meant. We gave her a piece of paper and pen so she could draw it for Ben. When Pascaline showed him the paper, Ben jumped up and started weeping. He went running from our hotel room in tears.

Pascaline asked me if she had drawn something bad, like a bad word. Brian and I didn't know what the symbol meant, but we couldn't imagine that God would show her something bad. Brian went after Ben to see if he was okay, if he wanted to talk. He told Brian he needed to be alone, and he'd see us at breakfast the next morning.

We came down to breakfast the next morning, and Ben was already there. His face was red and puffy. He'd been crying all night. I sat down next to him, and he said that he wasn't sure how to explain what had happened last night. But the symbol that Pascaline drew was a symbol his parents had given him, connected to his name and being. There was no way Pascaline could have known that. With tears in his eyes, he said, "I've been wandering the streets all night because I've always believed in God, but I never realized He knew my name. My name. And now that I know this, I know what to do."

Brian and I had no idea what that meant. We just knew

that God had spoken to Ben and showed Ben that God not only loves him but knows his name. That's what 4 Minutes is all about.

After we came home, I had a dozen articles written with photographs for Disney's parenting website. They were scheduled to be published over the next few months. Brian was editing the footage he had filmed. But did we really do all that God wanted us to do? After all, God had taken us to Egypt. He had given all of us the same word, *go!* He had divinely connected us with a tourism company that provided for a month of travel. There was no mistake that God had ordained this trip. And yet, I kept thinking about all the interviews that had been cancelled.

I remember sharing my worries with Brian one night. He looked at me and smiled. And then he said something I'll never forget: "Do you believe that God would send our family halfway across the world for one man? Ben always knew God existed, but he never knew that God knew his name until that night we listened for him. I believe God would do that—that He would send a whole family across the globe because He loves each of us that much. I know He loves Ben that much."

I remember Max Lucado once writing that God is like the hound dog of heaven. He never stops coming after us, finding us, letting us know He cares.

Throughout our travels in Egypt, Ben said he'd never leave Egypt. No matter how much Egypt was struggling, his family would stay. This was his country. Months after returning from home, we learned that Ben had moved his family to New Zealand. His wife is a Kiwi. That is what he knew he had to do after our prayer time with him.

A year later, we launched Adventure Family, our family

travel show that took viewers off the beaten path and inspired families to unplug and share adventure together. Disney and another network were doing the show together. They had a never-ending list of legal matters to agree on, but they finally agreed on one thing. They both knew they wanted us to start filming the show in one country.

You guessed it...New Zealand.

CHAPTER 10

How We Met Disney

How we met Disney is one of our craziest stories!

We didn't meet Disney because we were doing 4 Minutes. We met Disney in Tennessee because someone else had listened for us.

I was invited to speak at one of the largest mom blogging conferences in the country. About a thousand mom bloggers were coming to Tennessee from all over the country. The only problem was that I was already booked to speak for Sony at one of the largest portrait photography conferences in Vegas the week before. I've spoken at this conference several times for Sony, and I always leave completely exhausted. Brian and I would need to fly from Vegas to Tennessee to make the mom blogging conference.

When Alli called to invite me to her mom blogging conference, I had to decline. I couldn't do it in good conscious knowing I'd come empty and worn out. Alli understood. But a couple weeks later she reached out again to make sure I hadn't changed my mind. In fact, she reached out three times!

The third time we talked, she stepped out on a limb. I'll never forget our conversation. She said "I'm not sure how to say this. I'm not even sure where you are with faith and spirituality. This is not a faith-based conference, but I'm a Christian. And every time I pray about who should be here, I have a picture of you meeting someone significant."

Pray. Picture. I leaned in.

Alli went on to tell me that she wasn't trying to manipulate or convince me to come. She just felt that she needed to tell me about the picture. And then she ended with words like "take what makes senses and leave the rest."

I've been in Alli's shoes many times. I've prayerfully listened, and God gave me a picture for someone who I didn't even know well. I had no idea what their faith was or if they even believed in anything at all. And my whole heart didn't want to offend them. But I couldn't shake the picture I've been given.

Alli said, "Every time I pray about who should be here…" God wasn't going to let it go until she stepped out in faith and called me.

Well, I booked a flight to Tennessee. Of course! Wouldn't you?

I've asked this question to several people. And many have said that if they were honest they most likely wouldn't have gone. But because Brian and I had made a practice of doing 4 Minutes, pressing in to hear God speak, acting on what we were hearing for own lives, we were full of faith that He'd speak to someone else about us. That's the key. When you're doing the 4 Minutes consistently, you're open to hearing from God in all kinds of ways.

True to what I expected, I was drained physically and emotionally after the week of speaking in Vegas for Sony. I went to the airport, and they had printed my name wrong. (This was before smartphones and mobile boarding passes. Paper tickets, friends.) The attendant at the gate almost didn't let me board. By the time we made it to Tennessee, I was beyond exhausted. As I like to say, "I was shattered."

The next morning, I spoke to the mom bloggers. Everything went great. It was such a fun experience. Brian and I were mindful of who we were meeting or introduced to. A dozen major household brands were there looking for inspiring mom bloggers to partner with. Of all the new people and brands we met, none of them stood out in a significant way.

The conference had another day to go, but I was spent. We were also missing our kids after having been gone for more than a week already. I asked Brian what he thought about us heading home a day early. Crazy, right? We were there because Alli saw us meeting someone significant, but I couldn't stay another moment.

We headed to the airport in the afternoon. It was empty,

and there were only four of us going through security. Me, Brian, and two women trailing behind us.

For a number of years, Brian and I did a ton of travel for our business with photo shoots and speaking engagements. We decided early on to fly separately. One of our friends had lost both parents in an airplane crash when she was seven. Pascaline was about seven when she told us this story. It was all I needed to hear. From that day on, we never flew together.

It may sound like a lot of work to fly separately, but there were perks. Brian and I are together all the time. Like *all* the time. We run our business together. We homeschooled the kids together. We vacation together. Flying separately was the only time we weren't together. And I always got upgraded to First Class when I flew solo. That was definitely a perk!

Brian and I were once again flying separately this day but went through security together with only the two women behind us. He always tries to find ways to make me laugh. So he started to pretend like we don't know each other, flirting with me and trying to get me to say yes to having a drink on the other side of security. I'm like, "Oh my goodness, can you just push your bags through!"

Brian kept egging me on. The two women started laughing behind us. Now he had an audience. We got through security, and he grabbed me, double dipped me, and dramatically kissed me in front of the two women and security!

One of the women dropped her handbag and said, "Oh my gosh, you guys are married! I'm so depressed about my marriage."

She literally said that out loud.

Brian's flight was already boarding, so he had to take off. But my flight still had more than an hour before it boarded. I asked the woman if she wanted to have coffee and talk about her marriage.

We talked for an hour about everything from their communication, finances, intimacy, dreams, you name it. Toward the end of the hour, my flight started to board. I gathered my things and said, "I didn't even ask you what you're in Tennessee for."

She looked at me and smiled. Her next words blew me away.

She said that she had been at the conference I spoke at. Her flight was supposed to be the next day, but they had booked it wrong. She wasn't even supposed to be at the airport. Unbeknownst to me, she had heard me speak. And she was there undercover for Disney, looking for an inspirational mom to build a new brand and TV show around. "And I think I just found her," she said, looking right at me.

Two months later, Brian and I were flown to Disney's headquarters in Berkley, California. When we walked into their boardroom to meet with all the executives, everyone stood up and said, "Show us the kiss!"

There are so many pieces to this story that I love sharing about when I speak. But one of the biggest things I want you to take away from this is that you don't need a manager, an agent, or some other networking type person to reach your dreams when God is in your corner. He can open any door, any place, at any time. He can intersect your path with anyone you need to know. He just needs to know if you're willing to risk going on an adventure.

Remember the definition of adventure? We hear adventure and often think excitement or a remarkable experience. But Webster's dictionary has three parts to the definition of adventure. The first is "an undertaking usually involves danger and unknown risks." The second is "an exciting or remarkable experience." And the third is "an enterprise involving financial risk."

I think God was behind the order of Webster's three points of definition. Before you can get to the "exciting or remarkable experience," you first have to be willing to step into "the undertaking that usually involves danger and unknown risks." Going from Vegas to Tennessee was an undertaking that involved unknown risks. What if we didn't meet anyone? The "exciting, remarkable experience" wasn't a guarantee. Taking any type of adventure involves danger and unknown risks. Taking an adventure with God, the God who is for you and not against you, is going to provide a remarkable experience. The third piece of "an enterprise involving financial risk" I'll get to in another chapter.

I'm so thankful Alli stepped out on a limb and told us what she was picturing every time she prayed for her conference. She didn't have a picture of me meeting Disney. There weren't any words written in the sky that a show with Disney was going to come from it. All she got was a simple picture of me meeting someone of significance.

That's how God often works with the pictures we get for others. It's never the big three of quitting your job, meeting your spouse, or hearing it's a boy or a girl. And if you ever think it is, restrain from sharing it.

You know it's God if the picture, word, Bible verse, or

sense you're getting almost feels too simple. It almost makes you uncomfortable to share it because you imagine the person saying, "And? Go on." But that's it. That is all you got. You're afraid to look silly…another great indicator that God is speaking to you.

Because Alli was faithful to share her picture with me, not knowing what my faith even was, I met Disney. Brian and I developed an amazing partnership with Disney for the next several years, producing a show that I hosted called "Capture Your Story with Me Ra Koh." I went around the country teaching moms and kids how to capture photos of the people and things they love most.

For years I've had a following of three- and four-year-olds who will call out my name and come running whether I'm in Costco, the airport or Central Park in NYC. The show airs several times a day on Disney Junior, and the kids want to show me all the photos they've been taking with their parents' phones. It is the best!

I think about being a young girl growing up in Eugene, Oregon. My Korean dad was one of the only minorities in town. After school, I'd watch Sesame Street. I loved Maria. Even though she was Hispanic, I related to her. She could speak another language. She had olive skin with dark hair and eyes like me. Maria was one of my first women role models.

My prayer is that our Disney show has brought joy and inspired creativity to the millions of moms and kids watching. That they feel God's love coming right through the screen. Millions have watched the show. It's hard for me to even fathom. All because one woman took a risk and shared a picture she saw when she was praying.

Imagine what can happen when you share the simple

pictures you're getting for others. Millions of lives could be reached through the most unexpected, playful way.

CHAPTER 11

One Way Tickets to New Zealand

L et's talk about that third part of Webster's definition for adventure: "an enterprise involving financial risk."

Our partnership with Disney was going great. The VP executive we were working with loved our family. She asked if there was another type of show we'd be interested in doing with the family.

Ever since the kids were four and seven years old, we'd been going to Thailand once a year. We'd take three flights, a taxi, and a rickety, long-tail boat ride to our destination. We'd jump out of the boat with our backpacks of clothes, camera gear, and homeschool books, as we waded to the beach. Our open-aired jungle house was home for four to six weeks every year. I could write a book on all the adventures we experienced as a family throughout those ten years of going. That's what we wanted to inspire families to do—to unplug and take an adventure off the beaten path.

The VP loved it, but there was one problem. Disney's whole brand was centered around the messaging of "Don't take a risk. Come to Disneyland where it's safe, clean, and the happiest place on earth." Having our jungle home ransacked by forty monkeys on a regular basis wasn't exactly the same kind of messaging. But she wanted this family travel show to work, so she reached out to another network to partner with. Disney would help fund the production, and this other network would air it.

Our kids were ten and thirteen at the time. As a family, we started doing the 4 Minutes about this idea almost every day. The vision started building between the four of us. Instead of doing a temporary trip, we saw ourselves going to several countries. We had a picture of us putting our Seattle home on the market and everything we owned in storage.

I started freaking out.

I loved our home. It was five blocks from the water, twenty minutes from my parents, forty minutes to my younger brother and cousins. Everything I'd ever known was there. To uproot with no idea of where we were going or when we'd be back terrified me.

Brian was the opposite. The show was his vision. One night in a hotel room in San Diego we started arguing about doing this family travel show. I told him that it was asking too much of me. Why did we have to sell our home? Couldn't we just come back? But that's not what he was sensing from our 4 Minutes.

Feeling like we were both at a dead end, he shook his head and said words that changed everything. Brian assured me that we wouldn't do anything drastic, like selling our home, unless we both had peace from God. He also said that he'd spent our whole marriage empowering my vision with photography, speaking, and writing books. And he loved it and didn't regret any of it, because when we got married his vision was to support me in any way possible. But this was the first time he had a tangible vision that he needed to pursue. "I feel like I've modeled for Blaze what it means to be a husband who supports and empowers your wife, but I haven't shown him what it means to be a man who is unafraid to build my own dreams too."

God was so thick in that hotel room. Something started to shift in my heart. I was still afraid and wanting to hold on to security and familiarity, but I saw the importance of taking this adventure with God and Brian.

We found our cameraman Kevin. After filming in Egypt, we realized that if we didn't have a second cameraman besides Brian, it was going to look like a single mom traveling with her kids. Nothing wrong with that, but that wasn't our family makeup. Between Brian and Kevin, they would do all the filming and audio production. Brian and I would be the producers. It was a tall order, something we'd never done, but we were determined. Every time our family did 4 Minutes, our vision only grew and grew.

The two networks and their lawyers went back and forth for months trying to agree on something that would get us going.

The one thing they could agree on was that they wanted us to start filming in New Zealand. Since we'd never filmed and produced this kind of show, they felt like an English-speaking country would be one less hurdle to deal with.

More months went by, and our family was filling up our prayer journal with daily 4 Minute words and pictures. We knew if we didn't leave soon then the show would have to be postponed for a year because winter was coming in New Zealand. But in the TV world, what seems like a good idea now can be irrelevant in a year. Brian and I knew we had a big decision to make. Do we go without a contract and trust that God was going to work out all the details? Anyone who has ever done TV would be shouting, "You're out of your mind!" And they would have good reason.

The one thing that we kept coming back to in our family's 4 Minutes was that time we all got the same word. The word *go*. That was almost two years ago at this point. But we didn't have enough funds to take our family of four and a cameraman to New Zealand for a month of filming. So we decided to try a Kickstarter fund. In less than two weeks, we raised $30K for our show called "Adventure Family."

The funds paid for all our audio equipment, extra equipment needed for filming, as well as five one-way tickets to New Zealand, food for the month, and airfare to the next country. But we would have to have our signed contract and first payment before we left New Zealand. At least that's what we thought.

We weren't even sure where to go after New Zealand. So we bought one-way tickets and put our home on the market and all of our belongings in storage. Without a contract, just a promise from the VP at Disney that she'd get it worked out, we left everything we knew behind. Webster writes that the third way to define adventure is "an enterprise involving financial risk." Which we definitely did with one-way tickets. We boarded Air New Zealand with only enough money to film for a month, armed with cameras, microphones, and a journal full of pictures and words our family had heard in our 4 Minutes.

When we landed, we got word from the VP that negotiations weren't going well. Brian and I sat in the back of our RV and panicked because we had put everything on the line, and now we weren't even sure if we should be filming. We wondered if we should focus on getting paid photography gigs in New Zealand. What was the more responsible thing to do? We weren't in our early twenties backpacking; we were parents with two kids and a cameraman.

So we did our 4 Minutes in the back of that RV. The question we put before God was "What do we do?" Blaze had a picture of a volcano erupting but people on the island weren't scared, just going about normal life. I felt like even though things were scary, we didn't need to be scared. I knew that was God, because as a mom I was terrified of what we had gotten ourselves into. As a family, we decided to film the show in faith.

If you've never been on camera before, one of the toughest things is that you can't hide anything from the camera. But my emotions ranged from "this is completely irresponsible as a parent" to "this was exactly what we should be doing." The camera caught all my emotions.

During the first couple days of filming, Kevin hit pause on his camera after I said a bit about bringing the family to New Zealand. With eyes full of kindness, he said, "Me Ra, you're telling the camera this is the adventure of a lifetime, but you look absolutely terrified."

It wasn't an option to spend the next four weeks faking it. So what did we do? Brian and I went back into our RV and did the 4 Minutes again and again until I could become fully present with trusting God for this single day. Tomorrow was tomorrow. Today was what we had to focus on.

The temptation was to do other things then what we had come for. With no guarantee of the contract and funding coming through, I wondered if we should let our newsletter and social media know we were available for family photo shoots in New Zealand. There was nothing wrong with that idea, except that it took us away from focusing on what we'd come to do.

We did our 4 Minutes in the back of that campervan several times a day. It strengthened our focus to be present and believe this is what we should be doing. When I was on camera, and my mind started spinning again, I remembered what gave me peace during our 4 Minutes. It took the verse in Joshua 1 that says, "Don't look left or right," to a whole new level of meaning. And like Joshua 1 says, "Give it everything we've got."

A BACKPACKER WALKS INTO A BAR

Every few days the networks reached out and said one of two things: "The contract is almost finalized. We should have it to you any time." Or they said the complete opposite: "We don't see this contract ever getting worked out." Putting our hope or despair in their updates was constantly threatening to sink our spirits. We'd do the 4 Minutes again, pressing in to have that picture or word that reaffirmed God brought us here, not a network.

I've never worked the muscle of faith so much in my life. Every day it got worked to the point of exhaustion. Every day it felt like we upped the weight. And after a couple weeks, my fears of making the biggest mistake started to transform into complete surrender and belief.

After our month of filming in New Zealand, we had a choice to make. We still didn't have a finalized contract. The networks' lawyers were still hashing it out. Do we go home, or do we keep going? And if we keep going, where do we go? Guess what we did? You guessed it! We did our 4 Minutes as a family again until we had a clear sense of what the next step was.

We bought one-way tickets to Thailand.

Before we left New Zealand, we had one more stop to make. Ben, our Egyptologist Guide who had become our friend, had relocated his family since we said our good-byes in Egypt. It had been over a year since we'd seen him. Our reunion was sweet and sacred. It started with "I can't believe we're on the other side of the world seeing each other!" And then the conversation went to the more vulnerable places of the heart. Leaving his country and all his family had been a difficult transition. Being reunited with us encouraged him that God had not forgot about him. God still knew his name.

We said our good-byes and headed to the airport with one-way tickets to Thailand. I don't advise buying one-way tickets. We were told in New Zealand that Thailand requires you to have a departure date when entering their country. But God hadn't given us one yet, and the fact was that we didn't have money for a departure ticket. The airline said that we could risk being detained in Thailand with fees up to $20K per person. My heart was really racing now. We boarded the plane with full awareness of the risk we were taking.

We landed in Thailand and went through customs. Thank God, no one asked us when our departure date was because we didn't even have enough money for accommodations. Our family went back to the area we'd been going to for ten years. Upon our arrival, a local friend told us one of the homeowners was so inspired by our family that they offered to let us stay as long as we needed. I wanted to fall on the beach crying. God had provided a place to stay.

Our family filmed all the wonderful things we love about Thailand's culture, nature, and people for a month. You can see all of our episodes if you go to our *Adventure Family* website, https://merakoh.com/AdventureFamily. As we filmed, the networks kept saying the contract was coming any day now...or never. We kept doing our 4 Minutes. There are so many great stories to share about this time that I'll have to share more when I come speak at your church or conference. But I do want to share one of my favorites with you about a backpacker we met in an open bar.

In this part of Thailand, all the bars are open-aired with bamboo platforms that sit above the sea. There is no age limit, so our kids were with us. We noticed a young man, a backpacker by himself. Let's call him Tim. Having traveled extensively, we know firsthand what it's like to be hungry for conversation with new friends. We invited Tim to join us. He told us that he was from the US, traveling alone for a couple months. There was a sadness to Tim that we couldn't ignore. So we asked him if our family could do 4 Minutes for him and explained what we meant. He nodded yes.

Blaze's picture is the only one I can remember because of the startling response Tim had. When it was Blaze's turn to share what he got, he looked at Tim and said that he was a little embarrassed to share. Blaze had just turned ten. Tim was super intrigued, he told Blaze he was open to whatever he got.

Blaze had a picture of Tim walking down the beach holding a girl's hand. This is the part that embarrassed Blaze because he could tell it was Tim's girlfriend. But then Tim let go of her hand and took Jesus's hand. And they continued to walk together for a long time. After a while, Tim and Jesus met another woman and Tim took her hand.

This twenty something backpacker had tears in his eyes and shook his head in disbelief. He told us that he had broken off his engagement before traveling to Thailand. It was the hardest thing he had ever done, but he just couldn't go through with it. And he had been searching for truth and faith ever since. Through this 4 Minutes together, Tim felt closer to God than ever before.

Our family filmed as much as possible, but we always looked for heads that were bowed—people who were desperate to know God knew their names and cared about their lives. We'd do the 4 Minutes for as many of them as we could, writing down all the pictures and words we got so they could continue to reflect on them after we were gone.

After a month, monsoon season started. Torrential rains made it impossible to leave our wet, open-aired home. We still didn't have a contract or payment from Disney or the other company. I looked at our bank account, and we were down to $200. It felt like we were always down to $200. For a month, our family and cameraman stayed under cover while the monsoon rains washed away our confidence in the next step.

CHAPTER 12

Stuck in a Jungle

S eeing the $200 balance in our bank account left us feeling completely defeated. We had no idea of where we were supposed to go next or how we'd even get there. Our cameraman was starting to wonder about us with good reason.

The kids were on the couch, and I looked at them and said, "Well, we can either look at this one of two ways. We're either stuck in a jungle, or God hasn't shown us what the next door is yet." They both smiled and said, "God just hasn't shown us the next door, Mom! Everything will be fine." Even though they were only ten and thirteen, they'd been practicing 4 Minutes with us for six years now. They had heard God's voice about coming, and they had faith for us being there. And I loved them for it.

A year prior, when we were doing our 4 Minutes about the idea of a family travel show, I had a picture of us being connected with an investor in Dallas. Even though we lived in Seattle at the time, I was so sure of this picture that Brian and I flew to Dallas and met with any type of investor we could find. None of the investors worked out, but a local church leaned in.

Covenant Church in Carrollton, Texas, was founded by the Hayes family. Their daughter, Amie, had become a dear friend over the years. She had us meet with her dad who was the Senior Pastor at the time. They loved our vision and the idea of having something inspiring for families to watch on TV. They weren't sure how to help but offered their editing team as a possible resource when we got to that part of the production. Their confidence in our vision was powerful. It planted the seed of us one day living in Texas, just to be surrounded by people of great faith. To them, our vision didn't seem impossible but completely possible! When you find these people in your lives, you find a way to stay near them. Just being around them can change your life for the better.

One morning while in Thailand, I got an email from Amie's brother. He was also a pastor at their church. His email was short and to the point, but I still read it a dozen times in disbelief. Stephen asked if we had time in our travel schedule to go to Israel. He was friends with a local Dallas, Jewish billionaire who needed some of his philanthropic work filmed. If we had time, he would pay us for it and be an investor in the show. Did we have time? Yes, time is all we had!

Three days later we left the Thailand's monsoon rains behind and flew to Israel.

We spent a month filming in Israel, learning about their culture, faith, and history. Our episodes on Ancient Jewish practices are some of my favorite. We also filmed a bunch of footage for Covenant Church's outreach to the locals and the philanthropic work of the investor in Dallas. It's always so inspiring to see what people are doing to make the world a better place.

During our time, our family had the opportunity to celebrate Shabbat with a Jewish family and community on the West Bank. Shabbat is the Jewish Sabbath that begins at nightfall on Friday and lasts to nightfall on Saturday. This community was made up of rabbis, bankers, poets, professors, and politicians. Most were from Europe or the US and had immigrated to Israel.

Jewish culture encourages kids to ask questions. Pascaline had a question after dinner. There were about twenty neighbors in the living room, and I'll never forget all of them growing quiet to hear Pascaline's question. She asked the rabbi if Jews believed in hell. He leaned forward with a smile and said, "That's a great question, Pascaline." Then he looked around the room and asked, "Who would like to go first?"

For the next two hours every one shared their different and often contradictory opinions. And sometimes the ideas would get pretty heated in the room. At the end, the rabbi thanked everyone for sharing and looked back at Pascaline and smiled. "Was that helpful?" he asked with a chuckle. "I don't think we really answered your question, did we?" He looked at all his neighbors who were still there and then back at Pascaline and said, "But I hope we've shown you that it's okay to ask a question that can be difficult for a community to answer and even disagree on. Even though we don't agree on one answer, we all agree that we are a community. And that the question is valuable." That experience shaped our family for the better.

The next morning at breakfast, the family we were staying with asked us more about our journey and what brought us around the world. We shared our 4 Minutes listening prayer practice with them, and they were fascinated. The rabbi's wife teaches Rabbinical Law in Jerusalem. She loved hearing about this practice as a family, and it encouraged her own spirit that God still speaks to creation today. They were excited to try it with their own kids. The 4 Minutes is not meant to be stuck within the four walls of a church. It is for everyone who desires to hear God's voice.

When we were done filming the show, we had just enough money to fly our cameraman home. He'd had the adventure of a lifetime. During one of our last dinners together, I asked him what he felt like he was taking away from his time with our family. He said that he got to witness what a healthy marriage can look like—even when under incredible stress. And he said that he had already called his youth pastor from years ago and was going to try church again. He had been watching our faith up close for a number of months now, and it was something he needed to search out more for himself. I couldn't have asked for a more wonderful, powerful response. Somehow in all our stress and daily battles with fear and doubt, our faith had still managed to inspire our cameraman and those we met along the way.

Our family didn't have enough money to fly home, but we had enough money to get us to Europe. We had friends living in Italy at the time, and they welcomed us to their home with open arms. I remember walking in their door and wanting to sob. We had just been on the greatest adventure of our lives, and it asked everything of us. I had nothing left. Our ten days with them was like a healing balm of rest and reflection that I will always savor.

Since we were done filming the show, I posted online that I was in Italy and available to do photo shoots. Our friends shared it with their friends. We booked enough families in Italy to pay our family's flights back to the US.

We came home to our empty house. It hadn't sold yet. And we had $15 to our name. Literally. We'd invested it all and still had no contract. It felt surreal to be back after such a huge adventure and still feel lost to what the next step was.

The next morning, our first morning back home, Brian and I sat in our empty living room wondering what to do. An email came from Disney with a contract. We couldn't believe it! Somehow God had provided for several months as we circumnavigated the globe with often only $200 to our name. And now the contract was finalized and in our inbox.

For the next several weeks, we continued to ride the roller coaster. A higher-up at Disney started firing the VPs whole team. But he couldn't fire her. She was able to fight for two more shows to get their funding before she left. We will always be in debt to her committed fight for *Adventure Family*.

The network Disney partnered with was in complete disarray. They didn't think they wanted the show anymore, even after the filming and contract was finalized. Brian and I started hitting the pavement pitching the show to anyone we could find. I pitched the show more than a hundred times. We came so close three times that we took our friends out to celebrate and bought them dinner. The third time, they wouldn't let us buy them dinner until the network was finalized.

I wish I could say we eventually got a network to air it, but we never did. After a hundred pitches, we felt God release us to let go. Some of the episodes were aired on different Disney distribution channels and this other original network. But the whole show in its entirety wasn't ever bought. Networks and sponsors either wanted us to argue more as a married couple, have our kids talk bad about each other, or talk about the sponsored brand like an advertorial—all things we weren't willing to do.

I can't tell you how many times I've asked God why He took our family on that journey. I don't feel like I have the whole answer, but I do feel like I have a partial answer. As parents we want to tell our kids they can do anything, to reach for their dreams. But how often do we model that for them? When Brian and I talked in that San Diego hotel room, we both agreed that we wanted to give our kids a front row seat to what it means to build a dream with God. There are major ups and downs. Sometimes you're downright terrified. Some days you're not sure how you're going to pay for tomorrow. But God always shows up. He always provides.

Whether it's a random homeowner in Thailand who gives you his home for two months, or a Jewish billionaire you've never met who proposes an offer, God always shows up. He is faithful. And He wants to take you on the most unforgettable adventure of your life. And to think it all started that one New Year when we all got the same word *go* during our 4 Minutes. Who would ever guess that setting a timer for four minutes and practicing listening could turn into an adventure around the globe?

PART 4

Thirty Years Later

CHAPTER 13

Speaking at the Largest Meditation Center in North America

A dear friend and fellow photographer invited me to speak at her annual creative conference. We don't share the same faith, but she has a deep respect for who I am and what I have to share. Her request was two-part: to do a three-hour seminar on how I got into photography and favorite shooting skills and techniques, and then to speak at the end of the conference on what sustains my creativity. The second part was wide open to how I wanted to approach it. The first thing I thought of was sharing our 4 Minutes practice.

As a working artist, we spend a lot of time creating in the unknown and struggling with the temptation to constantly second-guess what we're creating. It's not a hobby when your creativity is providing for your family. The temptation of playing it safe and getting a day job is always there. I know Brian and I would not have made it this far as working artists if it wasn't for the 4 Minutes.

Since 2007, when I became one of Sony's first two women photographers to ever be sponsored, I've done a lot of public speaking. Most of them are photography or creative conferences in nature. Some are women or corporate events. Every time I'm invited to speak at a church, I jump at the opportunity. It's wonderful to share my faith freely and openly with an audience that shares the same faith.

However, wherever I speak I often share parts of my story that I first shared with you in this book. Sony has been an amazing partner in always letting me be myself. But sharing our family's practice of the 4 Minutes as a speaker outside of the church walls is not something I had ever done before. And yet, every time I listened with Brian or by myself about what to speak on for my friend's creative conference, God kept bringing up 4 Minutes.

Wanting to respect my friend and her invitation, I called and asked her if it'd be okay. She was more than happy to have me be my authentic self and share from the heart. She said that the conference was at the largest meditation center in North America and attendees were artists coming from diverse lifestyles all over the world. My lifestyle was just as valid as any other. My friend is a true gem.

We had already moved to Frisco, Texas, by this time. I

asked my pastor and spiritual mentor if she would pray. She put me on a prayer list that went out to 1,500 prayer warrior women. To say I felt covered in prayer was an understatement.

As I drove through a torrential rainstorm into the Blue Mountains of North Carolina, I kept thinking that if anyone is meant to hear God's voice—like the out-of-the-box type of things—shouldn't it be creatives? We're already living outside of the box, pushing the limits of our creativity. Maybe I needed to not worry and see this as a wonderful community of artists who were open to the unknown and mysterious side of God.

Toward the end of the conference, I stood in front of a few hundred artists from around the world and shared a lot of the stories within this book. I told them about emailing Egypt, how much God loves Legos, and more. And then I did something I've never done before. I suggested we do the 4 Minutes all together.

My heart was racing; I had never done the 4 Minutes on this large of a scale. But I know human nature overcomplicates things, and I wanted them to see how accessible and powerful this listening exercise was. We needed a volunteer, someone we could all listen for. I honestly didn't think anyone would volunteer, and that they all probably thought I was nuts. But when I asked if there was a volunteer, before I could even finish the question, a woman jumped right up and came to the front.

I was shocked.

Hearts were open, and she was desperate to hear God's voice.

I asked her not to tell us anything about her life. We were going to set the timer and listen for her for four minutes. And that way, if we received anything that spoke to her, we'd all know it was God and not our imagination. Then I asked someone to set the timer for four minutes.

That was a big mistake.

It was the longest 4 Minutes of my life! Why didn't I just set my own timer so I could look at it if I needed to? Remember how I said in the beginning of this book that sometimes the 4 Minutes can feel like it goes by in seconds and other times it can feel like it lasts forever? I was convinced the person hadn't set their timer. I couldn't listen to save my life because I was so freaked out that ten minutes had already gone by! Somehow in all this anxiety, I got the word *water*. But that was it.

I debated on whether or not to ask the person if they set the timer, but then what if they had? Wasn't I supposed to be modeling this for everyone? There are no words to sufficiently describe how scared I felt. And then all of a sudden, the timer went off.

Everyone looked up. I asked for a show of hands if they felt like the 4 Minutes went by super-fast. Half the group raised their hands. I asked for a show of hands if they felt like the 4 Minutes went on forever. The other half raised their hands.

I shared the boundaries we practiced as a family. No future telling of whether or not she should quit or take a job, marry someone, or the sex of her future babies. The audience chuckled. This was all about sharing encouraging words, pictures, senses, Bible verses, or quotes that we felt we heard for her.

One woman volunteered to share first. When she was done, I asked the woman up front if what she said connected with her. She shrugged her shoulders and said she didn't really know. Nothing jumped out at her. I asked someone to be our recorder and told everyone, "That's okay. That's why we write it all down because some things don't make sense until much later. Some things never make sense. But you never know unless you write it down."

Someone else raised their hand and said they got the word *water*. More than half of the attendees, including myself, all said, "I got *water* too!" It was a complete hair-raising, powerful moment. God was in the room!

Then someone else raised their hand and asked if she could share her picture. The woman said she had never done a listening exercise like this and didn't really understand what she was seeing, and yet the picture she received was super clear to her.

She had a picture of the woman walking along the beach carrying broken seashells in her hands. An older gentleman approached her and started to walk beside her. They came to a stop and stood at the edge of the shore. The older gentleman asked her to throw the broken shells into the water. She didn't want to at first, but she finally decided to trust him and did.

As she threw each broken seashell into the water, the waves brought it back to her and the seashell was made whole. It was like it had never been broken before. The woman who had volunteered burst into tears next to me. Everyone was stunned. This picture meant more to her than any of us could even fathom. It took several minutes before she could stop crying. When she was ready, I asked her if she would share why the picture touched her so deeply.

The woman said that for ten years she'd had a vision of

something she wanted to do with her photography. But she was to afraid and had kept plugging away at her day job. The vision never left her. Every year it grew more and more within her heart. Until six months ago, she finally decided to quit her job and risk it all. Things had been going somewhat well. But in the last month, she struggled with a ton of doubt and fear, wondering if this was a big mistake. She said that she had been asking the universe for a sign to let her know she was going in the right direction. This picture couldn't be a bigger sign.

The audience and I were still confused, so I asked her how the seashells related to what she does. She looked at me with such kindness and then looked at the audience. She explained how she interviews victims of sexual violence, recording their stories to give them a voice. And then afterward she has them choose a gown and get into a pool where she photographs their rebirth underwater. The women were the broken seashells, and as they went into the water, they came back whole and reborn.

I wasn't the only one who started crying. God was so thick in that place—the largest meditation center in North America. I never wanted to leave. I told everyone that this was God speaking to us. Not the universe, but the Creator of all the universe.

I may never know the impact that experience had on the people who attended. But I know the impact it had on four of us. The woman who was brave enough to volunteer. The other woman who had never experienced having a picture for someone and now saw the impact of how powerful and life-giving it is to listen for someone else. The impact it had on me— this will always be one of the most sacred speaking engagements I ever experienced. And weeks later, I found out in an email the impact it had on a fourth person.

He had taken my photography seminar earlier in the weekend, and I remember him leaving abruptly halfway through. He didn't make a scene, but I felt something clanging in my spirit when he left. Something odd that I couldn't put my finger on. A couple days later, I saw him sitting in the audience again when I spoke on the 4 Minutes. He cried when the woman shared what she did for a living, and how the picture told her what her heart needed to know most.

Weeks later, he sent me an email and said that more than twenty years ago, he had sexually violated a girl in college. He had never told anyone. After hearing my story in the photography seminar, and then being at the last talk, he knew God was asking him to share with someone. Even though he was terrified, he went home and made an appointment with his priest. For the first time in twenty years, he confessed everything and felt an indescribable weight come off of him.

He then told his wife and experienced grace and forgiveness through her reaction. His email had a purpose. He wanted to know if I would stand in the place of the college girl that he had violated all those years ago so that he could ask for forgiveness.

I cried when I read his words. It brought up my pain, but I could also see his own pain. I shared his email with Brian. We prayed together, and I responded with Brian copied on it. I told him how much it meant to have him share something so painful. Standing in the place of the college girl, I forgave him. And I knew that God forgave him as well. He thanked me, and even though it was an email I could feel the tears of healing in his response. Since the conference, his whole life has changed. He is living in more transparency, his marriage is stronger than ever, and he has returned to church with the mentorship of his Catholic priest.

I have a feeling there are more stories from this conference that I'll hear one day in heaven. But for now, I can't imagine a more redemptive outcome. I'm so thankful for the 1,500 women at my local church who prayed for God to show up in a powerful way. He sure did. And I'm so thankful for my friend who invited me to come and speak. Even though we don't share the same faith, our friendship is sacred.

CHAPTER 14

Six Months to Hurry Up and Stop

*A*dventure *Family* had come to an end, and we were at a new crossroads of what to do with our business. We had started leading photography travel workshops and taking people to some of our favorite countries, like Italy, Greece, and Thailand. The question was whether or not we keep building up the travel side of our photography business, return to our grass roots of family portraits, or do something entirely different.

We were facing the great unknown again, and we were tired. As much as we love travel, our bodies were tired. Our family was also entering a new season where living nomadic wasn't as feasible. Pascaline was applying to universities, and Blaze was thinking about attending the local high school. That alone would ground us because we didn't want to be gone traveling all the time without the kids.

We'd experienced some amazing adventures with God. We were open to whatever He had next. After a few months of meeting with business advisors and wise counsel, and also doing our 4 Minutes, we had a new vision. We had spent almost two decades building a national brand, but now it was time to return to our roots.

We decided to open a local portrait studio in Frisco, Texas, with a mission to provide a fun photographic experience to bring families closer. Through our discovery process before photo shoots, we listen to what is most meaningful to clients and the ones they love. That's what we photograph and help clients display in their homes. Brian calls it "positive propaganda." They are the messages of truth about the love for each other that clients want to surround their families with every day.

Finding a beautiful commercial space to lease made sense. We were new to the North Dallas area, and we wanted to make a splash! Disney's Photo Mom was now here and excited to capture families! We started a six-month process to find and design a space with the backing of investors or an SBA loan.

Taking on overhead when we'd been working out of our home, sometimes even suitcases, felt scary. We did the 4 Minutes almost every day throughout that six months. And every time we did the 4 Minutes, we felt renewed with deep peace to keep going forward.

We were within a few days of signing on the SBA loan

and the commercial lease when we did the 4 Minutes again. And out of nowhere, we felt God ask us to wait. I can still picture Brian's face, his shock mirroring my own.

"Was that really God?"

"Set the timer for 4 Minutes again?"

The word was *wait* again. If you've done paperwork for lending and leasing, you know that you're trying to get all the stars to align within certain dates. And if those things don't line up, everything can fall apart. Getting the word *wait* meant that we were going to let go of the last six months of work with the SBA and the property. Why would God bring us all this way just to not have us take the last step? And what were we going to do in the meantime?

The next day, we pulled out of signing the SBA loan and said good-bye to the commercial space. Brian and I knew that we couldn't move forward without that deep peace we'd come so accustomed to receiving, especially with a decision as big as this.

Without a commercial space, we decided to transform our upstairs into a studio space. I'm not really one who struggles with ego, but in all transparency, I was disappointed. I wanted our brand to make a splash on the North Dallas/Frisco scene. A beautiful space felt glamorous and exciting! A home studio felt like the opposite. But the more Brian and I talked about it, we reminded each other of how our hearts love to inspire others. Having a big, beautiful space right out of the gates wasn't that inspiring to intimidated newbies in the photography industry. But anyone can start a studio out of their home.

As the months went on, unexpected storms came. Grief

and loss hit my heart in multiple ways. My beautiful grandmother who was always such a big part of my life went home to be with Jesus. She was in her mid-forties when I was born, and our birthdays were two days apart. I had celebrated my birthday with her for as long as I could remember. My heart grieved for months after she was gone. If we had leased that commercial space, she would have passed away the second month of our studio opening. Looking back now, I can't imagine going through that deep grief while also trying to launch a new studio with overhead we weren't used to.

A couple months later, we had to put our golden retriever, Rosie, down. She had been with our family for twelve years. I never realized until she was gone how much her big sighs and tail wagging filled the empty space throughout the day. That same year, a good friend passed away from cancer. Her diagnosis came as a shock, and within five months she was gone.

The biggest grief of all was our daughter getting ready to leave for college. The months leading up to her going undid me as a mom. As you've read, our family has spent so much meaningful time together. I couldn't imagine our family with her being away at college. I cried every day for months, my heart grieving a season in our family that was coming to an end.

God knew all this was ahead. He knows how much we can handle. Having a home studio gave me space to grieve, move slower, and not stress about paying extra overhead. I thought I needed the studio space; God knew my heart needed even more space.

We also met a wonderful business coach to help us with the specific type of business model we wanted to grow—one that brings families closer together through helping them discover what is most meaningful in their relationships. Steve's mentorship and heart commitment to help us has been profound. We've learned so much. Looking back, I can't imagine opening a commercial space without his guidance. God knew we needed more expertise to build something long lasting that would have great impact.

WHIPLASH WHEN GOD HITS THE BRAKES

It's shocking to be running in stride with the Holy Spirit, building our impossible dream, and then all of a sudden have God hit the brakes. My spirit experienced whiplash. But as time went by, God started giving us revelation, little by little, on why He hit the brakes.

A year later, COVID happened. When quarantine went into effect, Brian and I thanked God that He hit the brakes with us on leasing a commercial space. I can't imagine the stress that would have been. Honestly, I've lost track of all the times Brian and I have looked at each other and said, "Wow, I'm so glad we didn't go forward with that SBA loan and space."

Six months into COVID, one of the Dallas Cowboy NFL players became a client. I felt the temptation to feel embarrassed that we had a home studio. But he and his wife were so gracious. After we showed them all the "Best Of" portraits for their photo shoot, he smiled big, looked at Brian and I, and said, "This is really cool. This whole experience is really amazing." I wanted to cry. He didn't see all the things I felt like we were lacking in having an impressive, commercial space. We gave our all, and that is what gave so much to him and his wife. In the next couple weeks, we had two more Dallas Cowboys book photo shoots!

As small business owners, creatives, and working artists, there are always a hundred voices telling you why your business isn't "ready enough" to go for it. Hesitation is the constant battle. Second-guessing is the ongoing mental dialogue. We want all our ducks in a row before we really put ourselves out there.

I wanted a beautiful commercial studio space because I told myself that would qualify us for higher-end clients. But God doesn't work that way. He asks us to give Him our two loaves of bread and five fish because He wants to do something magical, powerful, and unforgettable. He wants to multiply the little we have—so little it seems insignificant and lacking—and He wants to multiply it. Why? He wants all the glory.

Brian and I have talked with a lot of young people over the years who are struggling to hear God's voice. They want to know which direction to go before they take the first step. For us, we've always chosen to step out, trusting that God will stop or redirect us if we're taking time to listen. I love how Proverbs says that man makes his plans, but the Lord directs his steps (16:9). But to have your steps directed, you have to put one foot in front of the other. If you are open to Him redirecting you, you don't have to worry about walking the wrong direction. He'll straighten out your course.

I share this story with you as an encouragement. Brian and I have been practicing the 4 Minutes for almost thirty years. We spent six months diligently listening, believing we were getting the green light the whole way, just to hear "stop" at the last moment. But God promises that nothing is in vain when we are walking in step with Him. Even when things don't make sense.

The six months of doing all that paperwork for the SBA loan wasn't a waste. When you apply for an SBA loan, part of the process is submitting a thorough, detailed business plan from marketing to financials for the next five to ten years. Even though we weren't going to move into a commercial space right away, we now had a map of how we wanted to launch the business. And now we had a new vision! We didn't want to only lease a space, we want God to give us the funds to buy the space!

When God first hits the brakes, and your spirit feels that whiplash, it's easy to think it was all a waste. But give it time. Keep doing the 4 Minutes. Ask Him for revelation. As the weeks and months unfold, you will see how He had your back the whole way. And the dream isn't over; it's only getting better.

CHAPTER 15

The Waiting Room of God

S ometimes the 4 Minutes is about creating space for grief.

Imagine standing on a beach with your little ones. Grief is rolling toward you like the waves. The kids don't see it. They just want to splash in the water and play in the sand. Their joy is overwhelming. Unbeknownst to them, it heightens your pain. You feel empty and a storm within is stirring, but you want to be stronger for them. What you don't realize is that if you give yourself permission to grieve, you will be.

We only need to be on social media for five minutes to

feel the pressure to make the most out of COVID-19. Pascaline was telling me about a post that said something like, "If you haven't written a book, learned a foreign language, started a new business idea, or lost weight during this time, you have no excuse." I beg to differ.

The excuse that is real and worthy is found in the waiting where grief often lives. My friend texted me a powerful quote this morning:

"To us, waiting is wasting. To God waiting is working." –Louie Giglio

My heart identifies with that quote. Throughout my life, I have lost much. In times of grief, I have set my timer for 4 Minutes and found myself entering the "Waiting Room of God."

There is nothing to hurry with grief. It's more of a sacred space in waiting. Waiting for the pain to not hurt so much. Waiting for the loss to not feel so immediate. Then scrambling to hold on to the pain and loss because that is all you have left of the one you love.

In the Waiting Room of God, I've memorized all the cracks in the ceiling. The elevator music is on repeat. People have come in after me, and somehow they have also left before me. Sometimes I've wondered if God has forgotten my name is also on the list. That I need to see the Healer too. But I'm in a tug of war with healing. I want healing, but I don't want to move on without the one(s) I love.

Maybe it's not the death of a loved one. Instead, it's the death of expectations or disruption to our rhythm of life. Any unwanted or unexpected change warrants permission to grieve.

THIS IS WHEN I MEET GRIEF

Grief is like a favorite aunt with no agenda. She enters the waiting room and sees me sitting in the far corner. Instead of sitting next to me, she leaves an empty chair between us, because grief creates space. That is the gift she gives. She acknowledges the need for space while validating my need to not be alone.

She doesn't ask me how I'm doing. Grief just sits with me, waits with me, and holds a space for the pain—the empty chair between us. That empty chair gives me permission to grieve.

So many losses have sat in that chair. At 19, when I locked myself into a psychiatric ward, my pain sat in that chair. When Brian and I miscarried our second child, Aidan, all our lost hopes and expectations for him sat in that chair. When my grandmother died, I couldn't open my eyes because I felt her so close in that empty chair. When my oldest left for college, I felt part of my identity as a parent sit in that chair.

Dreams I have poured everything into and never came to pass have sat in that chair. Unanswered prayers I have relentlessly pressed into heaven have waited in that chair.

You see, we don't enter the Waiting Room of God alone. We enter with every loss, and they all deserve a place to sit. Even though others can't see them, their presence is more than real to us. That's why grief leaves the chair between us empty.

WHAT TO EXPECT FROM GRIEF

Productivity is praised so much in our society. But it isn't allowed in the Waiting Room of God. This isn't a space to find the silver lining or hustle at a new level. This is a place to set the timer for 4 Minutes, be still, and wait for God to answer. But this goes against our culture and our very nature. The mental battle begins. Are we wasting time in this Waiting Room of God? Or is God actually working on our behalf, and we just can't see it?

In a split second, loss is triggered. I can be having a great day, and then all of a sudden, I see a woman who reminds me of my grandma. I hear a mom call her son Aidan. Or I walk into Target, and it's decorated for Valentine's Day—the anniversary of being date raped thirty years ago. With every unexpected trigger, I am given the permission to grieve. Here's what I've come to expect from Grief:

- When Grief visits, it's always unexpected.
- Grief makes me tired. Not immobile or unable to function but very tired. I tend to need more sleep and struggle to focus until the grief passes.
- Watching a movie is an appropriate thing to do when grieving. The heart and mind need breaks too.
- I know Grief will visit me for the rest of my life. At first, I used to fight against this. But now I see her coming as a chance to remember the ones I've loved and the expectations I had to let go.
- Everyone's timeline for grief is different. And it often lasts longer than we expect.
- Grief mobilizes me. Depression immobilizes me.

THE DIFFERENCE BETWEEN GRIEF AND DEPRESSION

I've met many people who are afraid to grieve because they confuse grief with depression. Over the years, I've experienced both and found differences between the two. Instead of a favorite aunt coming to visit and sit beside me, depression barges into the Waiting Room of God. It tells me I "should" feel different. Grief has never used the word *should* with me.

Depression tells me I'm weak for being back in this spot. Grief is always available and never rushes me. Depression tells me I'll be stuck here forever and feeling the pain will only cause me to sink deeper and deeper. Grief tells me this too shall pass, and when I embrace the pain that activates the passing.

Lies come with depression. Depression tells me no one cares. I'm failing my family, myself, and my business. Grief tells me that not everyone understands, but I'll have more to give the ones I love because I understand pain more. Depression tells me that at some point I'll never remember the pain, so if I do remember it, I must not be any better. Grief is always honest. She says I'll always remember the pain on some level because I loved so deeply, but in it I will also find my strength.

I wrote this chapter for you to give yourself permission to grieve. Sometimes that is what our 4 Minutes are for.

I see you on the shoreline afraid to wade into the waters. Maybe you've tried wading in and been crushed by the breaking waves. As our pastor once said, the shallow water is a dangerous place to stay. In the shallows, you get tossed around and knocked down and swallow a ton of water. But when you dive into the waves, pushing past the breaking point and into the deep…everything changes.

You can float on your back in the deep. The waves roll through you instead of over you. Even the storm clouds bring a refreshing rain that cleanses you. When you are ready, you flip over and leave the surface to dive down into the deep where mysteries wait to be discovered and understood. Where everything is quiet.

When your heart is heavy with grief, it's time to set the timer for 4 Minutes. To listen and honor what you hear. Let's go to the Waiting Room of God together. Let's keep the empty chair between us until the Healer calls our names. Let's dive into the waves and swim out past the shore.

THE MAILWOMAN ASKED ME THE MOST PROFOUND QUESTION

For ten years I passed her every day on her mail route. We would wave to each other during my morning walk. She was an older Chinese woman. We never talked much more than hellos. And then one day she stopped and said, "Is it okay if I ask you something?"

I looked at her and smiled, having no idea what she wanted to ask.

"Of course," I said.

"I don't even know your name, but I have to ask you this. Why do you keep fishing in the shallow waters when you know that the only thing that will sustain you is found in the deep?"

I was speechless. My heart quickened and leaned in.

"In the deep, the fish are much larger," she said. "But the water is colder, and it's darker. Harder to see. That's why we're afraid of the deep, but you don't have to be. You were meant to swim in the deep waters. You were never meant to be afraid of the dark," she finished.

My chest physically shook from the tears that started to pour out. It's like she was an angel who had been watching over me all these years. Before seeing her that day, I had been walking for the thousandth time, asking God if we should sell our home and film a family travel show. For two years, I did the same morning walk and asked the same question. I was in the Waiting Room of God—waiting for that deep peace and confirmation to come. And the least likely person, the mailwoman, is who God used to call my name and bring an answer. I went home that day and told Brian I was finally ready to risk it all.

EMBRACE THE WAITING

If you're in the Waiting Room of God, embrace the waiting. Don't give up and leave before the Healer calls your name. Wait with your pain, loss, and unanswered prayers. Keep the empty chair next to you. See Grief's kind eyes, filled with patience and gentleness.

You are not alone. It's okay if you don't learn a foreign language, start a new business, or lose weight. To hear the Healer call your name, the way you need to hear it, even through a mailwoman, is better than all those things combined.

One of the shortest verses is one of the most powerful to me. John 11:35 says, "Jesus wept." His close friend Lazarus had died four days prior. If you've read the story of Lazarus, you know Jesus raises him from the dead. So why did He weep beforehand? There are many schools of thought on this. Some say Jesus was weeping because of the people's unbelief. But that sounds like an impatient, judgmental God. That's not the God I know and serve. I believe He wept to create a space for their grief. In that moment, He made our own grief worthy. Before there was any hope of a silver lining, Jesus validated the pain.

If you have lost a loved one, give yourself permission to grieve. You are worthy of it. You are loved.

If you are grieving the loss of expectations and uncertainty, allow those things space in that empty chair. You are a complex, beautiful soul that is worthy of giving yourself room to feel the pain. And if the elevator music in the Waiting Room of God is getting old, I love the song, "Take Courage" (https://youtu.be/r49V9QcYheQ). It's one of my favorite ones to play. The message of slowing down to take time to breathe is powerful.

CHAPTER 16

When Everything Falls Apart

For nine months, life was about helping Pascaline survive college rejections. She had quite the journey filled with pain, confusion, disappointment, and unexpected reward. Nine months later, we moved Pascaline into her dorm room. She became one of three women in a sea of men military cadets.

This new chapter was not what I expected for my girl. But I'm so proud of her! This was the most unexpected journey of twists, turns, frustrations, and surprises to finding her college.

Pascaline's story inspires me to keep dreaming big

because God always delivers the unexpected. She gave me permission to share her unusual journey in hopes that it may encourage you to reach high with your own dreams.

Most college freshman start in the fall. That's what we were planning for Pascaline too. She had applied to six incredibly competitive schools, most being Ivy League. When we found out she was put on Princeton's deferred list, we were so excited because our homeschooled girl was in the running! Then the spring came. She got one rejection slip after another. Not one school accepted her, and she was devastated.

After two years of working so hard at the community college to finish high school and her first two years of college, she had maintained a 4.0 GPA with hopes of getting into one of her dream schools. And since she didn't apply to any safety schools, she had nowhere to attend in the fall.

As parents, Brian and I kicked ourselves for not pushing her to apply to a safety school. Brian and I felt completely helpless as parents. There wasn't anyone to call or a connection we had that could give her a place to start in the fall. Was the issue because we had homeschooled her since first grade?

We were all confused. As a family, we had done 4 Minutes several times together throughout her college application process. Every time we listened about her applying to another school, we got nothing. It felt like we were encouraging her in the right direction. But when all the rejection slips came, nothing made sense. It felt like everything was falling apart for her.

Pascaline's always been super confident and goal driven, but I started watching her second guess everything and feel completely lost. Every Sunday at church people would ask her where she was going in the fall, and I'd watch her struggle to answer. My spiritual mentor encouraged me, saying we want our kids to go through challenging times when they're home. This way we can help walk them through it. I held on to this wisdom as my heart broke for her.

All the rejections came within the same ten days. For the next three days, she stayed in bed and grieved. Brian and I were also teaching a workshop for two days, which gave her alone time to just be. She had bought the book *Principles* by Ray Dalio and thought that if anyone knew about disappointment, he did. She started reading the introduction and was blown away by his story.

He had bet everything and lost it all overnight. His company went from several people on staff to just him and needing to ask his father-in-law for help to pay the mortgage. Pascaline said that he went to a regular state school and majored in Engineering. Then he went to an Ivy League school for his MBA. She connected with the way his brain processed and shared information. For the first time she wondered if an engineering major was something to consider.

At the time Pascaline was considering being a Liberal Arts major interested in Art History, maybe even archeology or writing. But to apply to Princeton and Yale, you are required to take calculus. She was dreading the class but took pre-calculus and did okay. However, when she got to calculus I something clicked for her. She enjoyed it so much, she decided to take calculus II as an elective at the local community college. (Who does that?) And to our shock, she got 100s on her tests!

I'll never forget Pascaline coming down the stairs after those first three days of heartbreak. She told us what she'd been reading, and this idea of maybe majoring in engineering instead. Out of all the fields in engineering, the one that captured her interest the most was aerospace engineering. And the best universities to get major in aerospace engineering? In Texas where we were living!

When we met with her advisor at the community college to restrategize where to go for college, he looked at her course work and was confused. He said, "Even though you're a humanities major, all your electives are engineering based." We were all surprised.

Brian and I don't come from families of engineers. Both our dads were entrepreneurs. Yet we had been encouraging Pascaline to consider studying something she couldn't learn from her family. We just had no idea how different it would be! A new path opened up to becoming an engineering major. And the field that her brain enjoys most is aerospace. (I still can't believe I'm writing this about our daughter!)

The funniest part of this story is that out of all the subjects we did for homeschool, the one we struggled the most with was science. We did such a great job teaching the kids history, English, speaking, math, art, etc. But science…we just weren't into it beyond earth science and the animal kingdom. Sometimes I'd feel guilty about us not making more of an effort, and as Brian and I would get into bed, he'd say "Me Ra, it's not like our kids are going to become rocket scientists!"

In only a few short weeks of hearing she wasn't accepted into any of those other schools, she had a whole new vision. She applied to Texas A&M's competitive School of Engineering and was accepted!

She also decided to join the Corps of Cadets. They are

the largest, public military college teaching leadership program. Since there aren't many women in the engineering field, she thought the Corps would be an amazing way to learn how to not only lead but also specifically lead men.

That is how we ended up moving her into her first dorm room as one of three women in a sea of men to start her "hell week" of training at A&M's Corps of Cadets with the Navy/Marine squadron.

Did we hear wrong when doing our 4 Minutes about her college career? At one point, we were sure that we had. But looking back on everything, we're all in awe. It definitely wasn't a straightforward path; nonetheless, it was clear that God's hand was guiding her every step of the way.

She never would have known about her passion for engineering if she wasn't required to take calculus when applying to Princeton and Yale. Isn't that amazing? God gave her a big vision, and even though she thought acceptance to those schools was the end goal, He had something so much better in store. What looked like a dead end of how to survive college rejections became a new beginning. She thought she failed, but she fell into His amazing plan!

There are so many other amazing confirmations that fell into place as Pascaline moved forward with this new plan. We looked back on our New Year prayer journal from earlier that year, before she had received all the college rejections and even considered aerospace engineering. What's so crazy is that all three of us had pictures for Pascaline that entailed rockets somehow! We had no idea why! We even laughed about it and figured the whole thing was metaphorical. Little did we know that four months later, her life path would dramatically shift. And she could have confidence going forward knowing those words and pictures came from a 4 Minute time months before.

Just to think that God moved us from our home and all our family in Seattle, Washington, to Frisco, Texas, five years ago. He knew back then that she would be attending one of the best aerospace engineering schools in the country. He knew what we could afford and not afford. He knew it all.

Before Pascaline made her final decision to attend Texas A&M, she spent a night with the Corps Cadets. She came home from that experience and immediately asked if we could all do a 4 Minutes together. As a mom, I wanted to cry. Our kids are now young adults. They have the freedom to make their own choices about how they exercise their faith. All Pascaline wanted was to do 4 Minutes as a family. She said, "This is such a big decision. And I know that if we do our 4 Minutes, even when it gets tough in the future, I can look back to this moment and know I didn't make the wrong choice."

The house is much quieter with Pascaline away at college. Even though Blaze is still here, it's odd to have him at school every day after years of homeschooling. When Pascaline left for college, he thought it might be fun to try high school.

Brian and I sometimes joke that we already feel like empty nesters. What a change to go from traveling the world as a family to opening a local photography studio and having both the kids gone. But it feels so good, so right. They're building their own visions now. Together, as a family, we've learned what it means to adventure together with God. We've experienced the confusion of feeling like we heard from God, only to be confused, and then months later see it all unfold. I'm so thankful for those trials, as hard as they were. They gave the kids grit to keep believing, even when the evidence was against them. And Brian and I will keep doing all that we know to help our kids hear God's voice as they find their way four minutes at a time.

CHAPTER 17

Protection from the Storm Within

My girlfriend, Amie Dockery, told me a beautiful story about a practice shepherds did with their sheep. In ancient times, shepherds made their own anointing oil for their flock. With herbs and spices, they created their own signature mixtures.

They did this for two reasons. If their sheep ever got mixed into another shepherd's flock, they would be able to identify their sheep right away by the smell.

Secondly, the herbs and spices also had medicinal properties. Picture the shepherd pouring the oil into his hands and then massaging it into the sheep's wool around the head and ears and down the front legs. Amie said there is a microscopic mite that travels up the front legs of a sheep and enters the ears with a goal to breed and colonize in the ear canal and burrow into the brain. The oil kept these mites from attaching because they would slide right off.

"What gets in our ears eventually gets in our head," said Amie. "When this happened, the shepherd saw immediate change in behavior of the sheep. A lamb that would typically go to the shepherd for comfort would instead run off and act crazy, going against its nature to be protected."

The pain from these infestations would be so unbearable that the sheep would bang their heads against rocks, sometimes breaking their skulls, just to be free of the madness.

Who wants to be free from the madness right now? Who needs protection from the storm within?

Psalm 23:1 says, "The Lord is my shepherd; I lack nothing." Verse 5 in this chapter has always confused me: "You prepare a table before me in the presence of my enemies." How can I enjoy a feast when my enemy is breathing down my neck? When fear is screaming at me?

But then it says, "You anoint my head with oil; my cup overflows." Tears flow. That's how I can sit before my enemies and enjoy the table He's prepared. His anointing oil keeps the taunts, fears, and worries from burrowing into my brain.

Verses 2–3 say, "He makes me lie down in green pastures, He leads me beside quiet waters, He refreshes my soul." I close my eyes and picture God looking over His flock and seeing me. With kind, patient, loving eyes, He sees me. Bending down before me, He takes the anointing of His words and massages them gently into my head and ears. This is the magic that happens when you do the 4 Minutes.

His truth protects me, keeps me focused, comforts me in the middle of a raging storm. Because of this practice, I will not go crazy. Fear will not drive me insane.

When I was 19 years old, I checked myself into a locked psychiatric ward for a month. I know firsthand what it's like to feel like I'm walking a fine line of madness and reality.

I remember our early years of marriage. Even though I'd been through a lot of counseling, I still had relapses where I felt like I was going crazy. There was so much emotional pain to still heal from. When I'd break down, the only thing that felt calming and good was Brian holding my head firmly in his hands, as the whirlwind of fears calmed within.

Fear is relentless. Just like the parasites that burrow into a sheep's brain, fear burrows into our brains. If we aren't careful, it will drive us mad. We need protection from the storm within.

I have a lot of history with fear. That is why I talk about overcoming fear so much. This is why I depend on the 4 Minutes. I know what it's like to be a slave to fear. More importantly, I know what it's like to be set free of it.

Everyone is having to readjust to a new daily life with COVID. Parents are having to manage doing school with their kids while also working from home. It's completely overwhelming, especially when you're new to it.

Small business owners are having to pivot quickly to find ways to stay afloat. We're in that boat now. Worst-case scenarios saturate the news. Isolation magnifies the fears.

Every morning I wake up and read my Bible. It is not enough for me to pray. Sometimes my prayers of doubt and anxiety can add speed to that whirlwind of fear. I have to refresh my mind and heart with words of truth.

I love the Bible App BiOY (Bible in One Year, https://www.bibleinoneyear.org). Our family has been reading it for more than a year. Each day you are given a passage in the Psalms or Proverbs, Old Testament, and New Testament. There is always great commentary to go with it.

After I read my devotional, I often set the timer for 4 Minutes by myself. I let Jesus rub his anointing oil into my ears so I can hear the Shepherd's voice.

Let me encourage you to create a morning ritual for yourself. This will give you protection from the storm within. Even if you have to wake up an hour before your kids get up. Whatever it takes to set the timer for 4 Minutes, bask in the quiet, close your eyes, and see the Shepherd catch your eye. Watch Him come to you, bend down, and anoint you with His truth.

We are His sheep, and He is our Shepherd. "He refreshes my soul. He guides me along the right for His name's sake. Even though I walk through the darkest valley, I will fear no evil, for You are with me. Your rod and Your staff, they comfort me...Surely Your goodness and love will follow me all the days of my life, and I will dwell in the house of the Lord forever" (Psalm 23:3–4, 6).

CHAPTER 18

The Truth about Fear and Doubt

By now you've read some of our family's favorite stories—stories that have shaped who we are. You would think I never struggle with fear and doubt any more. You would think! But because my daily struggle with fear and doubt is so real is why we've done the 4 Minutes for so many years.

There is one benefit to Fear and Doubt: they remind me of how much I need Jesus. I love how Nicky Gumbel wrote, "Without doubt, faith would not be faith" (Bible in One Year). I used to think that I would achieve this level of faith where fear and doubt no longer impacted my day. Instead, I've come to accept that fear and doubt are committed to sharing their opinions with me for the rest of my life. Some mornings, before I've even opened my eyes, I can hear them sitting next to my bed talking. Fear is reminding Doubt of all the things I need to be afraid of for today and the next thirty years to come. And Doubt is overwhelmed by all the things there are to second-guess about any decision I make.

Even as I finish this first draft, my thoughts are already being tugged on. How will our studio manage this coming month? Will we make it through the fall and winter?

It's comical, right? I just finished writing a book of all the ways God has shown up for my personal life, marriage, family, and business, and I'm still struggling with Fear and Doubt about tomorrow. I hope you feel comforted by that reality. You are in good company. That's why Brian and I do the 4 Minutes. We need God's peace re-anchored in our hearts again and again. Sometimes it's every day, a few times a day, especially in seasons like COVID-19. Other times, we're in that wide-open meadow exhaling, taking in the beautiful view.

Fear and Doubt, they are committed suckers. I don't know about your life, but I know they're committed to my life for the long haul. They come on every journey with me, even though they're never invited. But the difference is that they don't call the shots. They don't sit in the driver's seat. I do. I love how Bob Goff writes in *Love Does*, "Forget having Jesus take the wheel. Get Him in the window and keep pointing at Him."

With every dream, every impossible mountain that Brian and I have faced, I've looked out on the horizon, squinting my eyes, trying my best to see what's up ahead. Sometimes all I can see is Fear and Doubt dancing along that horizon line. They see me looking ahead, and boy, do they get excited. They jump, shout, wave their arms, doing all that they can to let me know they're already there and waiting for me. Sometimes they're intimidating, and other times they're downright annoying.

But here's the truth about Fear and Doubt. Every time Brian and I get to that place of overcoming the mountain to build an impossible dream, we look around and guess who didn't show up for the celebration? Fear and Doubt! They are nowhere to be found. The only time they disappear is when we pause in our journey to give thanks, celebrate what we've done, and set the timer for 4 Minutes. It's like those things steal all the oxygen that Fear and Doubt need to survive.

Brian and I have climbed a handful of impossible mountains throughout our marriage. Some of them you've read about. Others I hope to share in future books. Our faith has been tested again and again. But every time we start building a new dream, I still struggle. The moment I set off into the unknown with God, Fear and Doubt are back again. Sometimes I remember to take breaks and set the timer for 4 Minutes, knowing it will scare Fear and Doubt away. Other times, I forget about 4 Minutes and get bullied.

The goal in life isn't to obtain a level of faith where Fear and Doubt can't reach us. They'll always be able to reach us on this side of eternity. Instead, the goal is to cultivate a practice of learning to pause, no matter how threatening the circumstances and odds. To set the timer for 4 Minutes. If we need more time, we reset the timer. Brian and I do it all the time. We wait for that deep peace to fill us, the kind that passes all understanding and changes our world. Once we grab hold of it, it's time to help other people find that deep peace too. That is how we change the world together.

Choosing to listen is a battle. Setting the timer for 4 Minutes can seem like a waste of time. But I hope the stories within these pages have given you a desire to try. Fear and Doubt may keep taunting us, but we don't have to be bullied by them.

MY BATTLE CRY

When I turned forty-five years old, I wrote the following post on Instagram. It poured out of my heart, and I've reread it several times since. It's become my battle cry for myself, my family, and you.

Society tells us lots of things about getting older. Here is my truth:

My forty years of wandering in the desert are over! I know who I am, and I know why I'm here. I've endured more hardship and loss than I can share. But I'm not bitter. I'm more expectant than ever! My years of tears have been transformed into years of laughter.

I feel more childlike than ever, yet I'm also a warrior. When the battle cry goes out, I stand ready to fight. I'm no stranger to the enemy. I was born on the battlefield where dreams, hope, and faith fight to survive. This is my home, and I don't plan to give it up without a fight. I stand in the gap for others to win. My battle scars are my evidence of unwavering, creative courage!

Confidence is my sword. Truth is my shield. Creativity is my strength. The Waiting Room of God, that I have spent endless years in, has transformed me. It has become a vast cellar deep within me. It is filled with large barrels of vintage wines.

Every prayer gone unanswered, every loss I've endured, has created rich, potent wines that are ready to serve when needed. Fit for a King.

My days of pain are not in vain. My childlike dreamer is fierce. I choose to embrace the messy, playfulness, unknown of creativity. I run to the next forty-five years with high expectations. I no longer live in shame but have removed all the veils. When I look at you, I look with all my heart. And I let you look inside me too.

My children know God's voice. They are kind and bold dreamers. My husband is a man of valor and endless humor.

Fear and Doubt wave to me on the horizon. But they are not creative or new. They are predictable and boring. I take my eyes off those two and focus on today, here and now, not looking to the right or the left.

I claim the promise.

Strength!

Courage!

God, my God, is with me every step I take.

Today, this year, and all to come. I am thankful. Even today, we birth a new beautiful chapter in our life and mission. May it fill you with joy and wonder!

CHAPTER 19

Let's Try 4 Minutes Together

Even though this book has come to an end, our conversation has just begun. Brian and I would love to hear your 4 Minute stories! We want to hear about the pictures you get, the things you're sensing, how it's encouraging or guiding you, and your questions. There is nothing more rewarding then hearing that this book inspired you to try 4 Minutes by yourself, with your spouse, kids, or friends.

Doing 4 Minutes is going to feel weird at first. As I said in Chapter 1, it's going to feel too simple. You'll be tempted to discard it after a few times of trying. But, remember, this is a listening prayer practice that takes practice. Learning to hear God's voice takes practice. The only way to get better at something is to practice it. As a working artist for more than twenty years, I know that every time I learn a new technique it feels awkward, messy, and almost like a waste of time. Try not to judge your first efforts. Trying something new is always awkward.

LET'S TRY IT TOGETHER

Why don't we end this book with giving it a try together? First, grab a journal so you can write down everything you get. As soon as you can, buy yourself a specific 4 Minute journal. For now, any journal, notebook, or blank paper will do.

Find somewhere quiet where you can sit and not be interrupted. Over the years, I've tried 4 Minutes while on my morning walk. And it just doesn't work for me. I think it's because I'm too distracted by all the information I'm processing from the neighbor's dog barking, to waiting at the crosswalk for the car to pass, etc. This practice has always been most successful in a quiet place, where I can just sit and listen.

Set yourself up for success on this. Silence your phone. Tell your spouse, family, or roommates that you're going to be in your bedroom for a little bit and you don't want to be interrupted. Maybe you're at work, and your heart needs to do this right now. Head to the bathroom. I've done 4 Minutes in bathroom stalls several times, whether I'm on the road traveling, about to get on stage to speak, or feeling overwhelmed and needing to retreat for a brief moment.

Now that you're sitting in your quiet place, think about

what is heaviest on your heart. Is it a broken relationship that needs healing? Something with your finances? Do you need direction on what to do with your kids? Is your business struggling? Whatever it is, pick one thing. That's what we're going to put before God in the 4 Minutes.

HOW WE ALWAYS START

Brian and I always read Joshua 1 from *The Message*. Let's read it together, refreshing our hearts with the truth that God is for us and not against us. Reminding our spirit that this 4 Minutes we're about to do is not a waste of time but life giving. When we get to the two parts where it says "Strength! Courage!" throw your first into the air to rally your spirit;

It's all yours. All your life, no one will be able to hold out against you. In the same way I was with Moses, I'll be with you. I won't give up on you; I won't leave you. Strength! Courage! You are going to lead this people to inherit the land that I promised to give their ancestors. Give it everything you have, heart and soul. Make sure you carry out The Revelation that Moses commanded you, every bit of it. Don't get off track, either left or right, so as to make sure you get to where you're going. And don't for a minute let this Book of The Revelation be out of mind. Ponder and meditate on it day and night, making sure you practice everything written in it. Then you'll get where you're going; then you'll succeed. Haven't I commanded you? Strength! Courage! Don't be timid; don't get discouraged. GOD, your God, is with you every step you take.

And then Brian often adds this last part, "Lord, give us ears to hear, eyes to see, and wisdom to understand what you want to share."

Hit start on your timer for four minutes. Come back here when the timer goes off.

REFLECTIVE QUESTIONS FOR AFTER

How did it feel? Did the 4 Minutes go by fast or slow? I often find that the first three minutes are often a struggle to stop my mind from thinking about every problem I want to solve. It's almost always that last minute, even 15 seconds, when the noise stops, and I hear or see something.

Sometimes it's the exact opposite. The moment I close my eyes the oddest picture pops into my head. I have no idea what it even means until I share it with Brian, and he shares his picture, which becomes the other half to the puzzle.

Other times I don't get anything, but I do feel a deeper sense of peace that wasn't there before.

What about you? What did you get? Write it all down in your journal. Is there a specific word that stands out to you? Perhaps spend time Googling that word. Sometimes more revelation will come. Maybe it wasn't a specific word, but it was a type of butterfly, flower, metal, rock, you name it. I love to dig a little deeper when I get things like this.

As you write down what you got, no matter how insignificant it may seem, ask God to reveal its meaning as you're recording it all. Sometimes the revelation comes during this part of the process. Does it remind you of a Bible verse you once read? Or maybe you can do a search for verses in the Bible around the word or feeling you got.

If you're doing this with someone else, take a moment to

share with each other. I've lost count of all the times Brian or one of the kids got something that brought meaning to what the seemingly insignificant thing I got. Sometimes each person in the family gets a piece to the puzzle. Sometimes just two of us do.

There are plenty of times when we didn't hear anything. That's okay. It's still worth writing the date down and "Didn't hear anything but feel more _____." How would you fill in that blank? Peace, hope, strength, lighthearted, or maybe more tears come up, more pain is on the surface, and your 4 Minutes did the powerful work of making room for it so healing could come.

Whether you sense, see, or hear something amazing or seemingly insignificant, God is working. As you continue to press into Him, He will teach you more and more about how you hear his voice. The more you do this practice and write your results down, you'll start to see consistencies in how you hear, what you see, how you feel. This is where confidence starts to grow. But it can only happen if you take the time to practice 4 Minutes again and again.

WORDS, PICTURES, AND SENSES FOR SOMEONE ELSE

If you feel like you got a word, picture, or sense for someone else, go through the checklist of boundaries we talked about in Chapter 1 before you share it. And most of all, is it encouraging? Our golden rule is to always encourage and confirm what they're already sensing. That doesn't mean we have to understand what the picture is that we got. Remember the lady I prayed for in church? I had a picture of her sister dancing with Jesus. I didn't know if she had a sister or how that would encourage or confirm what she was going through. But common sense told me it was a life-giving, beautiful picture.

When you get something troubling, sit on it and intercede. There are many words that I've received for another person, and I've never shared it with them. If the picture isn't encouraging or confirming, I know it's because God wants me to pray for them, doing battle on their behalf through prayer, even though they don't know it.

Sometimes I'm unsure of whether or not to share it. That is when I bounce it off of Brian, tell him everything and see what he thinks. If he feels I should wait and continue to sit on it, I do. Having a spouse, friend, or mentor you trust to share things in confidence with is a gift. If you don't have this spiritual, kindred spirit in your life right now, add this to your prayer list. Ask God to bring you one. I know He will because He desires for us to be in spiritual community.

JUST THE BEGINNING

The more you do the 4 Minutes, the more questions you might have. In the following pages, we list our contact info so you can reach out to us with any questions. We also have a website where you can access video content on me and Brian teaching on 4 Minutes for your marriage, family, church, small groups, business, dreams, and more. Thirty years into this, we're still learning all the time. We love sharing all that we've learned to help you discover that God knows your name and cares for you.

We weren't meant to walk through this life alone. If you're looking for spiritual community and kindred spirits to practice 4 Minutes with, join our community. God has so much to say to all of us. Let's encourage each other to set the timer one more time, and one more time after that, and one more time, until we see Him face to face.

Acknowledgments

The adventures you read about were manifested through setting the timer for 4 Minutes, acting on what we believed God was saying, and the love and support of some amazing people.

I want to start by thanking my husband, Brian. Even though my name is on the cover, we wrote this book together over the last thirty years. A number of years ago, Brian met me in the living room after the kids were in bed. Pouring us each a glass of wine, he asked me a single question that changed everything, "If we could create our own family culture for the four of us, what would it look like?" The book you hold is the answer to that question. I'm so proud of us, Brian. We started with nothing and built the stuff of dreams with our kids. Through heartbreaking storms and unfathomable mountain tops, we held on to each other. Thank you for always seeing the hope ahead, no matter how discouraged I would get.

Ryan Leak for pushing me to write this book. You have

always believed in the impact it would have on the church and those who are seeking truth outside of the church. I'm forever grateful for you.

The Hayes family for believing in our dreams and supporting them in practical, powerful ways. For your spiritual mentorship and bigger-than-life faith that has helped shape who we are and what we do.

To our Covenant Church family who always cheer us on, pray for my speaking engagements, and just love on us in the most beautiful, profound ways.

Heather, Rich, Jack, and Ben Mattera. Thank you for providing your special place in Colorado. When our family went, I had no plans to write this book. But there is something magical about your kitchen table and that mountain view.

Brooke Shaden, my creative soul sister, it is such an honor to press into the unknown alongside you.

To those special people who read the first draft and gave me such encouraging feedback: Misty and James Demelo, Amaryllis and Clint Hatton, Ryan and Amanda Leak, Licia Chenoweth, Anna Hansen, and Shalom Shreve.

My prayer warrior women and men who have been midwives to this process: my mom, Jay Acosta, Anthany Arosarena, Tebra Kolath, Johnny and Tiffany Montgomery, Ginger Bay-Anderson, Karen Baldwin, Jamie Kiles, John and Jenny Laurich, Dennis Mclure, our amazing Instagram followers, and the growing 4 Minutes Facebook group.

David and Nicole Binion, your friendship and those three dinners we went out to celebrate *Adventure Family* getting signed to a network, especially the third time when you said, "We can't let you pay anymore until the actual contract is signed." LOL! True friends!

Kelley-Ka Ritchie for being there when we washed up on Thailand's shore, believing in *Adventure Family*, and taking us deep into the culture and beauty of Thai people. Our family loves you!

Rachel, Matt, Emma, and Ryan McGinn, our family will never forget how you opened your home to us in Italy. We were so exhausted having been on the road for months. Our hearts were discouraged, bodies weary. You gave us your beds, cooked Italian cuisine for us, and listened to every story as we cried and laughed together. Words can't begin to describe how sacred those ten days were.

Margie, our time with you and Disney, creating shows together that inspire families was one of the most amazing chapters in our lives. We were meant to meet. Your friendship and champion of our creative visions has been an amazing gift. And we'll always have the airport story and "The Kiss" to trace it back to.

The Sony team and artisans whom I've had the honor of creating alongside for more than a decade. Thank you for always supporting who I am, how I create with the camera, and how I share it from the stage.

Deborah Benson, founder of Changemaker Talent, it's an honor to be a part of your dynamic, creative, talented speakers' bureau. Thank you for being so enthusiastic about this book.

My writing critique group: Emily Hilderbrand, Licia

Chenoweth, and Pascaline Tausend. Our monthly meetings these last couple years have been the most wonderful accountability to keep carving out time to put words on paper and craft the stories we carry.

Christi McGuire for your talented editing skills that have helped this book shine! I consider us connecting a divine appointment for a dozen different reasons.

Jasen Roman, your creative talent with this book cover is a gift! Your commitment to make every change is amazing. Thank you so much for helping us make this book a reality!

Our portrait studio team in Frisco, Texas: Angela Troy, Jenny McMinn, Ginger Bay-Anderson, and Cydnee Jex. The beautiful experience we cultivate and work to give every family spills out of all this. Thank you for being an amazing team that gives every client and family an unforgettable, transformative experience.

To my brothers, sisters-in-law, cousins, and all our beautiful kids. Halmoni and her early morning prayers influenced so much of my passion for prayer. I hope this book inspires all our little ones as they grow, knowing the great legacy they come from in Halmoni.

Both my parents and Brian's parents. For the last thirty years, you've watched us take some crazy leaps of faith. Even when you didn't know what to think (like taking your grandkids to Egypt right after the revolution), you always loved and supported us.

Shauni, you're the best baby brother, always listening and taking to heart what I'm going through. Your letters of encouragement while we were on the road filming meant the world. I'm so thankful for you.

Shae Min, you believed in us and *Adventure Family* with your whole heart, putting yourself on the line, making the most amazing introductions. You answered every time I called. Made me laugh even when I was crying. Thank you for never giving up on your big sis!

To our kids, Pascaline and Blaze, who have become the most incredible young adults. Dad and I always told ourselves that if we could teach our kids to hear God's voice, no matter what came your way, you'd be okay. Well, you're both more than okay! We wanted to give you a front-row seat to building a dream alongside God, so that when you built your own dreams, you wouldn't be thrown off by the highs and lows. We're so proud of the things you're dreaming for your own futures and how you practice 4 Minutes on your own. Most of all, thank you for blessing this book. It's a collection of our family's most sacred stories, and it means everything for you both to be excited for us to share it with others.

About the Author

Me Ra Koh is the author of half a dozen books inspiring the soul spiritually and creatively. She is a keynote speaker known for bringing laughter, healing tears, and powerful imagery. Koh is also a master photographer. In 2007, Sony invited her to be one of their first two women sponsored photographers. For almost a decade she hosted "Capture Your Story with Me Ra Koh" on Disney, inspiring millions of children and moms with photography. She is a regular go-to expert on *Live with Kelly and Ryan*, and her photography and writing have been featured in the *NY Times, The Huffington Post, Parenting,* as well as exhibited in the American Museum of Natural History, New York and Somerset House, London. She and her husband own a portrait studio in Frisco, Texas. With their team, they help families discover what means most to shine through their portraits and enjoy every day in their homes. They have two kids and love exploring the world with them.

Connect with Me Ra Koh

Me Ra would love to hear your 4 Minutes stories! Following your journey in learning to hear God's voice is one of her favorite things. Email your 4 Minute stories and any questions to mera@the4minutes.com.

For booking requests to have Me Ra speak at your next live or online event, contact her Speaking Manager, Deborah Benson, at Changemaker Talent, deborah@changemakertalent.com.

The 4 Minute Master Class

A few times a year, Me Ra and Brian offer a special 4 Minutes course where you get to dig in with them and see the 4 Minutes modeled. If you'd like to be notified of when the next session starts, please visit www.the4minutes.com and enter your email.

About Me Ra Koh Portraits

Families fly in from around the country to have their own Me Ra Koh Portrait experience. Based in Frisco, Texas, they are more than a professional photography studio. Through guided questions before the photo shoot, their team listens to discover what is special and important to you in this season. Their signature, collaborative process, results in custom fine art portraits and collections for your home and office. Your portraits are as unique and individual as you, your family, and loved ones.

Get ready for your Me Ra Koh photography experience! Rekindle the spark with your spouse, cherish your child's sense of wonder and boost your confidence. Their team will illuminate what means most to you because family is a work of art.

To learn more, visit merakoh.com.